GURNARD'S BOOK OF DELIGHTS

A Collection of Children's Stories

Copyright All Literary Rights: Gurnard Primary School, Vanessa Wester and S.P. Moss, 2013.

Gurnard Primary School, S.P. Moss and V. J. Wester have asserted their rights under the Copyrights, Designs and Patents Act 1988 to be identified as the authors of this work.

Formatting & Cover Design by Vanessa Wester

ISBN-13: 978-1490376684

ISBN-10: 149037682X

Thank you for buying this book. This book is licensed for your personal enjoyment only. All rights reserved. Except for use in any review, this book remains the copyrighted property of the authors and may not be reproduced, copied or distributed for commercial or non-commercial purposes without the consent of the author. If you enjoyed this book, please encourage your friends to buy their own copy. Thank you for respecting the authors' hard work.

Any reference to real names and places are purely fictional and are constructs of the author. Any offence the references produce is unintentional and in no way reflect the reality of any locations involved.

All proceeds raised from this collection will go towards GURNARD PRIMARY SCHOOL.

GURNARD'S BOOK OF

Delights

A COLLECTION OF CHILDREN'S STORIES

FOREWORD

At Gurnard Primary School we have always been proud of the children's Literacy achievements, which we believe to be strength of the school, so I was delighted when Vanessa Wester approached me to discuss running a story writing competition, as this would be a way to celebrate the children's work and share their skills with others. The result is "GURNARD'S BOOK OF DELIGHTS" which includes stories written by some of the children in an anthology, published alongside excerpts and short stories by professional authors.

Having now read the children's stories and witnessed their creative talents, I know my confidence in their abilities has been justified. There is such a wide variety of themes here, with the winners in each year group producing some fantastic storylines. I hope, as you read through this anthology, you will agree we have some very talented children, who may well grow up to become authors in the future.

Reading and writing are such important skills for life, by encouraging and motivating children to take an interest in these areas; we are providing them with the tools for the future. In turn this will enable them, as they grow to adulthood, to access and maximise the exciting opportunities in the work place and indeed in the world that will be available to them, many of which do not even exist at this moment in time.

Many thanks to Vanessa Wester and S.P. Moss for the time they have given to judging the entries and also to Vanessa who has given so generously of her time in compiling this – our first book of stories. I do hope you will enjoy reading the children's stories and who knows;

if this book is successful we could look forward to several more editions being published in the future!

Congratulations to all of the children who have had their work published – I am very proud of you all.

Liz Jackson

Head teacher – Gurnard Primary School 2013

TABLE OF CONTENTS

Reception (Ages 4-5)

KITTY GIRL AND BAD PUSS HAVE AN ADVENTURE by *Thea Tellick*

Year 1 (Ages 5-6)

THE DINOSAURS by *Fionn Buggy*
MR TIGER'S ADVENTURE by *Caitlyn Dexter*
THE PRINCESS AND THE GRUFFALO by *Esme Finch*
EVIE'S LOST BUILD A BEAR by *Evie Hippolite*
THE DARK KNIGHT by *Dylan Holley*
THE ROYAL BED by *Elsie March*
BELLE GOES ON A HUNT by *Caitlyn May Gillett*
THE GARDEN FAIRY by *Rosie Peters-Mairis*
THE RUNAWAY CAKE by *Charlie Sissen*

Year 2 (Ages 6-7)

DRAGON TIME by *Joe Cobden*

Year 3 (Ages 7-8)

THE MUD MONSTER by *Gabriella Hippolite*
THE TIME TRAVELLING BOY by *Cameron Hook*
THE MAGIC TALKING TREES by *Fina Ray Harris Bell*

Year 4 (Ages 8-9)

THE TOWER OF MYSTERY by *Beth Cobden*
PARADISE by *Bella Evans*
TIME TRAVEL by *Abbie Hartley*
THE TIME TRAVELLING TV by *Grace Roberts*
THE MAGIC GUINEA PIGS by *Erin Tellick*
LAZY MAZY'S REVENGE by *Elsa Wester*

Year 5 (Ages 9-10)

SHELBY AND THE PINK BOOTS by *Jessica Dixon*
THE ANCIENT TEMPLE by *Sophie Hartley*
THE ADVENTURES OF EINSTEIN'S CATS by *Beatrice Kirkby*

Year 6 (Ages 10-11)

TIME SLIP STORIES
By *Lily Ainslie*
By *Jacob Chapman*
By *Oliver Goddall*
By *Ben Jennings*
By *Chloe Long*
By *Izzy Spencer*
By *Ella Harmony Topping*
By *Michael Wester*

BONUS FEATURES

About VANESSA WESTER
DETECTIVE GLENDA by *Vanessa Wester*
About S.P. MOSS
THE TO-DO AT TESBURY'S by *S. P. Moss*
THE BROUHAHA AT BLUEY'S by *S. P. Moss*
Connect Online

KITTY GIRL AND BAD PUSS HAVE AN ADVENTURE

By Thea Tellick

Reception WINNER

Once upon a time there was two cats. They were called Kitty Girl and Bad Puss.

They found some lovely smelling purple daisies. As they smelled the flowers they were transformed back in time!

To the old days and they saw pirates. The pirates were searching for buried treasure. Kitty Girl and Bad Puss snuck on board the ship. It was very exciting

Just then, they went back again even further in time. This time they saw dinosaurs. Some were very big with long necks and lived in the swamp, they were Diplodocus.

Then they could see rainbows; one, two, three, four of them and they realised that they were back next to the purple daisies.

Goodness that was fun.

Just then a bee flew past. 'Hello,' she said, 'be careful of those purple daises, they are a bit strange!'

'Yes, we know, we just visited pirates and dinosaurs because we sniffed the flowers.'

Then the sky started to get dark, so Kitty Girl and Bad Puss went back home

THE DINOSAURS

By Fionn Buggy
Year 1

Once upon a time in my bed I had a dream about the dinosaurs. I wondered if I could go back in time. So, I went to get a Dinosaur truck. It took a long time to get there until I came.

I met a little dinosaur. He was eating some leaves when his mummy came back and picked him up quickly. So, I go past in my truck.

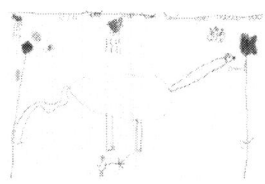

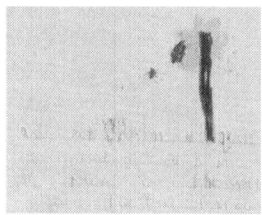

On the way, I saw big trees with coconuts on them.

And I saw something else… it was a spider! 'Ahhhhhhhh…'

I was scared so I smacked it when I got there.

Then I had my lunch.

After that I saw my friend, it was Joseph.

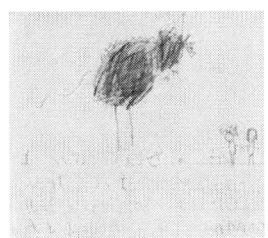

He went into my car and we saw a T-Rex! 'Ahhhhhhhh...'

We ran away.

So, we fell over smack. 'Ouch.'

'Shoo,' he said.

We jumped into our car. I drive into the desert. A scorpion came near me and said, 'Hello.'

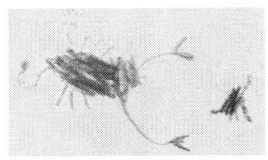

'Ahhhhhhhh...'

Joseph captured it so we could have a look at it.

Then the scorpion said something, 'If you will be good, I will help. You would like help?'

'Yes, we would.'

He showed us the way home.

MR TIGER'S ADVENTURE

By Caitlyn Dexter
Year 1

Mr Tiger was walking through the jungle one day when he saw a strange sight!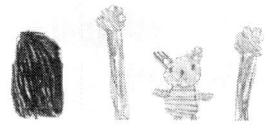

 There was a café in the jungle!

The café was in another time and place, through a hole.

Mr Tiger walked through the hole into the café.

He could walk and talk like a person in this strange café.

He had travelled through time and space and was in 3015.
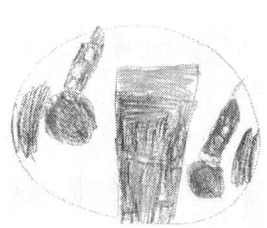

 In the café he met a lady Tiger and had tea and cake.

He took the lady tiger back to his home but she did not like it. She wanted to go back to her time.

Mr Tiger was sad but took her home and they had sausage and mash for dinner.

 Mr Tiger meets a lady tiger in a strange place.

THE PRINCESS AND THE GRUFFALO

By Esme Finch
Year 1

Once upon a time there was a little girl called Isabelle who liked walking in the wood.

She woke up in the morning!

Then she saw a Gruffalo. Then she ran away.

She went back home.

She went to her bedroom. She cuddled her teddies.

She sang to her teddies.

Then she told her teddies that she was running back home to see you since, 'I really missed you.'

Then out of her window she saw a Princess. She was very pretty. She had a very pretty dragon.

EVIE'S LOST BUILD A BEAR

By Evie Hippolite
Year 1

One sunny day there was a girl called Evie. She lost her build a bear, and she looked in the car and the van and her special box too, but she still couldn't find it.

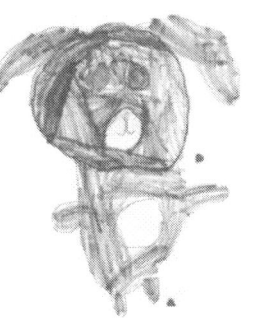

And the next day she went to the hair dressers and looked for it!

Luckily, this time she did find it.

She was extremely happy!

THE DARK KNIGHT

By Dylan Holley
Year 1

There was a little boy who was called Bruce Wayne. His mummy and daddy died. He grew up and became Batman. The boy wonder was called Robin.

He came to the Bat cave, but he had to leave.

The Joker was robbing the bank. Batman came through the glass roof and had a fight with the Joker, but when Tommy Two Face came through the doors, Batman was gone.

The next morning, Batman woke up as Bruce Wayne. Robin came through the door and Batman was having breakfast, but then turned into Batman.

Robin followed him, but didn't know where he was going.

Batman locked the door and went down the pole. He got into the Batmobile. Robin unlocked the door, but he was too slow for the Batmobile. Robin found the motorbike that Batman had made last night.

Robin rode the motorbike, but the doors to the Batcave were locked as well.

Meanwhile, Batman found Mr Freeze and a paper on the road. It said in the neighbourhood The Riddler was robbing the bank. Batman had a car chase with Mr Freeze and The Riddler was in Mr Freeze's car. Batman caught them and put them in jail.

Meanwhile, Bain wrecked Batman's car and Robin came from the corner and gave Batman a lift on the motorbike.

Batman and Robin got back to the Batcave, but they had lost the keys. Batman got a big hammer from the shop, but behind them was Poison Ivy. They had a fight with Poison Ivy. Poison Ivy got the hammer form Batman and hammered the Batcave to kill Batman.

Batman stopped being Batman and Robin became Batman.

THE ROYAL BED

By Elsie March

Year 1 WINNER

Once upon a time there was two Princesses: Princess Poppy and Princess Elsie.

Poppy had a time travelling bed.

They decided to go to the future to see what Christmas is like in 2013.

They arrived at *Busy Bees Christmas world.*

They bought some beautiful lights

to take home.

But when they got back to 1813, they realised they couldn't plug them in as there was no electricity.

BELLE GOES ON A HUNT

By Caitlyn May Gillett
Year 1

Princess Belle has got to find the missing Princess, her name is Anna.

Belle had searched the whole kingdom and couldn't find her anywhere.

The Queen told Belle to travel back in time.

Belle travelled back to the olden days in her carriage.

Belle looked everywhere, but couldn't find Anna.

Belle travelled back even further, but still couldn't find Anna.

The queen told Belle she might be going the wrong way.

Princess Belle travelled into the future in her carriage.

Everything looked different...

Belle spotted Princess Anna in a cage that the pirates had caught her in.

Belle rescued Anna and took her back to the castle.

The queen held a ball and they all lived happily ever after.

THE GARDEN FAIRY

By Rosie Peters-Mairis
Year 1

One day there was a Garden Fairy who looked after all the plants.

But, there was one problem... there was a cat who wanted to eat her!

She flapped her wings and flew. She flew into a closed flower and hid.

And the cat found her.

But, he was a friendly cat.

He wanted to ask her to be her friend and play with him.

THE RUNAWAY CAKE

By Charlie Sissen
Year 1

One day a mum and a dad.
The mum bake a cake.
The cake jumped off the plate.
The cake ran and ran.
The cake ran past T-Rex. The T-Rex has some babies.
The cake ran past some meerkats.
The cake met T-Rex, but T-Rex ran and ran to feed his babies.

DRAGON TIME

By Joe Cobden

Year 2 WINNER

One shimmering, starlit, night Joe was woken by a loud eerie sound. It was his dragon alarm clock. He had set it up because he was at a holiday cottage and was determined to wake up early and go exploring.

Silently, he crept to his mum's room and grabbed the key. Then he tiptoed down the stairs and unlocked the front door.

Outside, he strolled across the garden in semi darkness and found the same archway he'd noticed yesterday when they arrived, but it was glowing! He felt like he had butterflies in his tummy but he didn't care. Joe looked around him, then dashed through it.

Suddenly, the ground began to rumble. Then Joe felt himself falling as the ground around him gave away. Time raced past him, and he finally found himself in what seemed like another world.

Unexpectedly, what seemed like a wing grazed his neck. Confused, Joe looked up and discovered he was surrounded by loads of flying dragons! BUT, when he looked closely they were shivering, shaking and scared.

Joe thought it was because in the distance there was a

large dragon roaring louder than ever. He gasped, petrified, but the dragon didn't want to hurt Joe. He was in pain! Just then, the roaring dragon fainted and fell with a crash to the ground.

At first, Joe didn't want to go near him, but after a while he decided to approach the dragon. It was still breathing. He noticed that it had a spike in its toe. Joe grabbed the spike with both hands and pulled it out of the blue, scaly skin.

In an unknown language, the great dragon said, 'Thank you.'

Then with a giant clap of his wings Joe was sent back to his holiday cottage.

In his hands he had a blue dragon toy.

Joe ran home for breakfast.

His mum said, 'Hello what have you been doing?'

Joe said, 'nothing much!'

THE MUD MONSTER

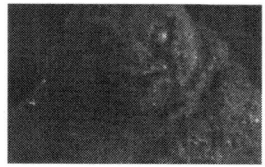

By Gabriella Hippolite
Year 2

Chapter 1: The Monster

One wonderful sunny day, there was a normal girl called Sarah. When she walks home, she walks past a swamp full of mud, but she didn't know there was a life threatening thing hidden in the swamp.

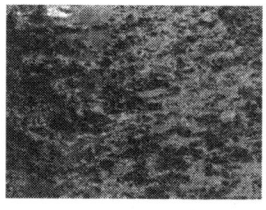

Then, one normal Tuesday, she was walking home. She was at the swamp when something absolutely terrifying jumped out of the swamp. It was a MUD MONSTER! She started to run back to school, but the mud monster caught up with her and grabbed hold of their hand. But, luckily her hand slipped out. She was perfectly fine except her hand was covered in sticky slimy mud. It was like frogs slime, but it was much worse.

Finally, she reached school. She felt like she had run a mile. She realised the monster was right behind her.

She was surprised she or the monster didn't slip over the slimy, disgusting mud. Then she ran into school. He followed her. She hid in the caretaker's room. The monster walked straight past her. Then she got out, but unfortunately he spotted her.

She then spotted the girls toilets. She went in, locked the toilet door when she was in, then she thought.

Chapter 2: The Plan

She thought of a plan. She needed to take a photo of the creature and show it to her friends, and then they will then of a plan to capture the mud monster. Then she quickly grabbed a camera from her class room. Then she saw the monster heading her way. Then she jumped out and took five photos.

Then ran as fast as she could, she felt like she was running faster than a cheetah or a lion. Then she finally saw the disgusting, slimy, swamp. Then she realised the monster was about a metre away. The she saw her doorway. She quickly opened it and rushed straight in.

Her mum and dad were still at work so she then locked the door and then looked out. To her amazement, the monster was gone. Then she heard some banging at the back door. She went to the very back of the house.

The monster was banging on the door.

Then she remembered the big, old fishing net. She ran as fast as she could upstairs. She went to the attic and got the fishing net; it still had some sea creatures on it.

Then she thought to herself, 'what about the other plan?' Then she said, 'Well, I have got an opportunity to do it, so I may as well.'

Then she quickly ran down the stairs. Then she opened the door and jumped, but missed the monster.

The monster started to run towards the school and the monster, just like Sarah, hides in the caretaker's room. Then Sarah walked straight past him, like the monster did to her, but then she heard the door creak. The she turned and she saw the mud monster trying to run out of the school. But, after five minutes or so, she caught up with the monster and then the monster turned round and saw Sarah with the net but it was too late.

The net was already in the air, and before he knew it the net was over him.

Chapter 3: Surprise, surprise

About an hour later, the monster found himself tied to a chair with a light in his face. Sarah was sitting opposite to the monster.

Then Sarah said, 'What are you doing here?'

Then monster said, 'I've come back from work to see you, Sarah.'

Then she said, 'Dad, why are you covered in mud?'

Dad then said, 'I fell in the swamp, then I was trying to tell you that and please can you untie me?'

Sarah said, 'Sure.'

Then Dad cleaned up and got some fresh, not muddy clothes, and Mum arrived soon after and everyone lived happily ever after.

THE TIME TRAVELLING BOY

By Cameron Hook
Year 3

There once lived a boy called Cam. Cam loved exploring so one day he set off for a walk in the park. But that walk to the park was not a usual walk to the park. He was trying to find something that he had not seen before.

On that day he thought he had seen a black hole looming in the corner of the field. So, he went a tiny bit closer and suddenly he realised it was a black hole. WOW! I didn't know they existed. So, suddenly he took a step closer, then he took another step and then in the blink of an eye he was swallowed!

Then Cam saw where he was.

He was in a submarine in the Atlantic Ocean and he saw lots of strange looking fish. And in that moment, he thought he heard a click.

So he went to the Captain, and said, 'I heard a worrying noise.'

So the Captain said, 'Don't worry.'

But, as soon as the Captain said, *'Don't worry,'* one of the submarines windows burst open!

Suddenly, everyone started to scream.

They thought they would not survive until a magic angel appeared out of nowhere.

The magic angel said, 'You will survive if you follow

these instructions. So, be wise and think. These are the instructions – stay calm and hold hands and you will start to fly.'

So, they did exactly what the magic fairy said and when they did hold hands they did start to fly.

They all shouted, 'It's a miracle!'

They said, 'Thank you,' and zoomed out of the water.

When they got out of the water, they said, 'Where shall we go?'

The Captain said, 'Don't ask me. I'm the person to blame.'

So, they all said, 'I think we should go to Greece.'

So, they said to their hands, 'Take us to Greece.'

They arrived in Greece after what seemed like a day, but it was only half a day. When they got to Greece, they did not expect it to look like an old dump site.

They let go of their hands and started to explore.

One of them said, 'I found a lizard lurking in a garbage bin.'

So, the other one said, 'I think we should go and have a look at that lizard then.'

So they all started strolling up the steep hill until they got to the little garbage bin.

'I think we should stroke it,' said Cam.

But, the others said in a big voice, 'NO!' It could have germs on it.'

So, the little boy stood back.

Cam said, 'Maybe, if we're careful, we could go a

little bit closer.'

So, they all said, 'Okay,' and took a step closer.

'Okay, now that's close enough. Now, I think we should leave this little lizard alone now.'

They began to walk up the hill even more.

Then, Cam said, 'I need to get back to my mum.'

But, there was something quite strange. There was a black hole at the top of the hill.

Cam said, 'This could be the black hole leading back to the park.'

So, Cam took a step closer. Then he took another step. And then, in the blink of an eye, he was swallowed!

When he got to the end of the black hole, it turned out that he was back in the park.

He went back down his gravelly road and got back home.

His mum said, 'How was your day today?'

Cam replied, 'Well, I can't really tell you, because you wouldn't believe me.'

THE MAGIC TALKING TREES

By Fina Ray Harris Bell

Year 3 WINNER

There once lived a girl named Sarah. She was very, very, very naughty indeed. She did not do as she was told. She argued for a long time. She was naughty at school and nobody wanted to play with her. Because she was so naughty she didn't have any friends at all. This made Sarah very, very unhappy, grumpy and miserable.

One day, Sarah decided to go for a walk in the forest. So, she went for her walk. When she got to the entrance to the forest there was a voice, but nobody was about... then there was a sparkle of dust!

It was a fairy, a very, tiny fairy!

The Fairy said, (in a very tiny voice), 'My name is Floris. I am 5 years old. Who are you?'

'My name is Sarah, and I am 11 years old,' said Sarah (in rather a loud voice for a tiny Fairy). 'My mum says I am naughty, but I don't think I am.'

The Floris said, 'If you want to be good and make your mum proud then follow me.'

So Sarah followed Floris.

When they stopped, they were looking straight at Unicorns, Fairies, Brownies, Sprites and Pixies!

Then Sarah said to Floris, 'I have never seen anything like this before!'

Then Floris said, 'I know, this is in a different world. This is where I live.'

Sarah said, 'Wow! This is a beautiful place.'

Then Floris whistled and two Brownies and two Pixies came along with a beautiful Unicorn. Its horn was glowing with magic. It was shining silver and its hooves were glittering with sparkles and there was no mud to be seen on this beautiful unicorn. The most amazing thing about this Unicorn was that it had two feathery, glittering wings that could fly high in the sky and swoop past the tops of the magic time talking trees.

Floris said, 'Sarah, you are going to fly on this beautiful Unicorn.'

One of the Pixies said, 'This little Unicorn is only a baby so be kind and gentle and help her by sitting still.'

Then one of the Brownies said, 'This beautiful sparkling Unicorn is called Starshine and she is very nervous.'

Floris then said, 'Right, Sarah, hop on to Sunshine gently and he will fly you two miles away to the Magic Time Talking Trees.'

So, on Sarah got and Starshine took her to the oldest Magic Time Talking Trees.

On the way, they were flying high above Baby Talking Trees and the wind was blowing in their ears! Sarah was a bit frightened, but she was so excited she just held her breath and closed her eyes. She did not have a clue what was going to happen or where she was going. All she knew was to hold on tight and sit still. Sarah was doing as she was told and not being naughty and being very kind, which was unusual for her.

When they finally reached two miles, Starshine said, 'Hold on tight because I am going to swoop down and let you get off to the oldest and most Magical Time Talking Tree.

So, Sarah held on really tight, trying not to hurt Sunshine. She tucked her head in Starshine's mane, while she was swooping down to safety on the ground. When Sarah opened her eyes and stepped off Starshine she gave the beautiful Unicorn a big cuddle and said, 'Thank you, Starshine,' and let out a huge sigh of relief.

Starshine said, 'Go over to that big, big Magic Time Talking Tree and say, 'please open up you doors and let me come in so you can show me how to be good.''

Sarah was a bit confused. She did not understand. But, anyway, she went over to the Oldest Time Talking Tree and said what Starshine wanted her to say.

When she turned around the most Magical Talking Time Tree said, 'You are most welcome to come in my doors.'

Then, to Sarah's surprise, Starshine was gone while she was talking. And all that she could see of him was a little gold footprint he left on the sky floor.

So Sarah thought of an answer for herself. So, she said, 'Okay, I will come in. So, if you do not mind, can you open the doors, please?'

So the most Oldest Magic Tree did as she asked.

When she was inside, the Magic Tree said, 'Close your eyes and clap your hands 10 times. When I say go, you start clapping. When I say open, stop. You have to stop clapping and open your eyes and you will be watching how children were told off in the olden days.'

So, when he said 'start' she did as he said. Then after about I minute he said, 'Open stop.'

She also did as he said and to her surprise she was watching 2 boys getting told off at school in the olden days. They had done something really bad and they got sent down to the headmaster to get dealt with!

They told the Headmaster what they did wrong and why they were sent to his office. The Headmaster grabbed the cane on the side of his desk.

Then the Headmaster said, 'Turn around and lay on that long table.'

So the two boys did as they were told and the Headmaster hit them both 5 times on the back and 10 times on the wrist and arm. Then the 2 of them started crying. Then they were shouted at to sit on the table and stop crying. But the Headmaster could not put up with it, so he sent them back to class still crying.

Then Sarah watched a girl and how she was treated, and how the other children were at home if they were naughty. This girl got angry because she was not allowed to go outside in the garden when it was raining.

Her mum said, 'No, you are not allowed outside in the rain, my dear.'

Then the girl said, 'If I want to go outside, I am going outside whether it is raining or not.

Then her mother said, 'Oh no, you are not. And by the way you cannot get out because the doors are locked.'

Then the girl said, 'Well, I have a different way of getting out.' Then she kicked the window, it smashed and broke into tiny pieces, and ran outside.

When her mum finally caught her she locked her in the spare bedroom with nothing at all. Her mother took all her money, made her give the whole town their newspapers for a week, and she had to have 50 cane hits every day for 6 whole months. Then she ended up with lots of bruises.

Then, after one and a half hours the Oldest Magic Talking Tree said, 'Stop and open.'

And Sarah said, 'Please, can you open your doors so I can get out.

Then the Oldest Magic Time Talking Tree said, 'Of course, my dear, I will let you out.'

So he did.

Then the Magic Time Talking Tree said, 'Whistle and Starshine will come and pick you up.'

So, Sarah whistled and there was a big flash of light, like a firework, flying across the sky!

Then Starshine landed on the ground and Sarah gave Starshine a big cuddle and said, 'I will never be naughty again, I promise.'

The Starshine said, 'Well, that is good. We will grab you in about 3 and 6 months' time and see. If you see a friend being naughty, scared, worried or anything like that then give me a call. All you have to do is whistle 5 times, clap 5 times and jump 5 times. Okay?'

Then Sarah said, 'Okay, I will. Now, please can you take me home?'

Starshine replied, 'I can't, Floris will do that. But, I will take you to Floris's house.'

Then Sarah said, 'Okay, let's go.'

So, off Starshine went back over the Baby Trees.

When they finally got back, Starshine said, 'Hold on tight, I am going to swoop down and land on Floris's drive.

Then Sarah said, 'Okay.' And she closed her eyes and tucked her head in Starshine's mane.

When they reached Floris's house, Starshine said, 'Go and knock on her door and say 'can I go home, please? I promise I will always be good.''

So, Sarah did, but first she gave Starshine a cuddle, a kiss and a big thank you.

Then Floris made a spell and made Sarah go back home.

When Sarah got home she gave her mum a big cuddle and kiss, and said, 'Sorry I am late for dinner.'

Her mum fell over backwards. In a shock, she said, 'Sarah, where have you been? Do not go away like that ever again.'

Then Sarah said, 'I promise, I won't.'

Then her mother asked, 'Sarah, have you been put a spell on to be good?'

Sarah laughed, and said, 'Why would you think that?'

Then her mother said, 'Well, you're acting very good and that's not like you because you're normally very naughty.'

At school the next day, Sarah was very good and was such a nice girl it was like she was a different person. And everyone wanted to play with her, and be her friend, and some even wanted to be her best friend, and wanted her to come and play and tea or even a sleep over.

Now, she was not a miserable, unhappy and grumpy girl.

She was an excited, wonderful, happy and joyful girl!

Everybody that knew Sarah was very, very proud of her now!

THE TOWER OF MYSTERY

By Beth Cobden

Year 4 JOINT WINNER

Oona woke abruptly and immediately thought, 'What a funny dream, why would there be a pony here?' Then she remembered where she was.

She was staying at her Uncle Alan's house, a small seaside cottage with roses and climbers smothering the white brick walls. The cottage was on the Isle of Wight, but at least it was not in London.

Next moment, Kasha screamed, 'Aaaaghh.'

Another nightmare!

It was their summer holiday and she had been to all the attractions her seven year old sister had wanted to visit, but today was Oona's choice.

Oona leapt out of bed, quickly dressed and ran into Kasha's room, 'Sis, SIS, are you Okay? I heard you scream'.

Kasha's face was colourless, her eyes blank with fear, her hair standing on end, 'The, the, the there w, w, w, w, were sc, sc, sc, scary things', Kasha's voice trembled.

'Okay, okay Kasha, let's go and wake Alan'.

Kasha jumped up in her nightdress and raced into Uncle Alan's room. 'I'll beat you,' she screamed from ahead.

Oona tutted, and ran along beside her sister and then shook Alan awake, 'It's my choice today!' exclaimed Oona.

'Alright Miss, can't a man get his sleep?'

'No', chimed in Kasha.

'Anyway,' hurried Oona, 'I choose to play in the moor.' She smiled with Kasha staring enviously, then moaning, 'Oooooh!'

'Come on Kasha, your sister needs a choice,' glared Alan, his words stinging like venom.

'Let's make brekkie,' suggested Kasha.

'Good idea', beamed Alan.

Oona charged downstairs and gulped her food down like a scavenger.

Straight afterwards, she ran out onto the moor behind the cottage, dizzy with a sense of freedom. But soon after she arrived, she felt an eerie silence and saw the sky turn an orange-purple with a hint of pink.

'Funny', thought Oona. She looked at the orchids and played with her dolls and was about to climb up a tree when... all of a sudden, a moor pony, obviously spooked, rampaged over. There was nothing she could do. She blacked out.

For a few moments Oona felt nothing, then her eye slowly flickered open, 'Where am I?' she thought.

A nine year old girl was leaning over her, 'Are you okay, Nicky?' exclaimed the voice.

Oona stood up dazzled. She managed to mutter a few words, 'I am not Nicky, I'm Oona.'

'Oh, how old are you?' said the unreal voice.

Oona looked around, miffed. There were no trees, no grass, just sand with a tower protected by sinister robots with red visors. There was no reply for a few minutes.

'I'm nine and a quarter. What's your name and how old are you?' asked Oona.

'My name is Eclipse and I'm nine and a quarter too!' smiled Eclipse.

'What's the date?' said Oona, still dazed.

'It's the fourth of November 31,' smiled Eclipse, helpfully.

'You mean the 21st century' reminded Oona.

'No, really, the 31st,' said Eclipse.

Oona's eyes bulged and her face turned white.

'Come on Oona, let's get you inside, I need to explain something.'

Eclipse dragged Oona to a cloud, who managed to say, 'Why is your bed a a a… oh nothing.' Oona lay on the cloud.

'Touch the wall,' ordered Eclipse.

'Why?' enquired Oona.

'Just do it OK,' ordered Eclipse.

Oona touched the wall, it felt like a school whiteboard. Then her hand felt like it had had an electric shock. The wall immediately turned green.

'Homesick, that explains it,' muttered Eclipse. She lifted Oona off the cloud onto a chair with wings, and then sat on a chair next to her. 'Why doesn't your top change colour?' asked Eclipse.

'No tops do, do they?' said Oona.

'Mine does, watch.'

Oona watched as Eclipse's top changed from blue, to pink to violet to green.

'Let me tell you, you have gone forward 1,000 years Oona. We are in the Tower of Mystery. It's called that because it's where we keep all of the world's books.'

'Why?' questioned Oona.

'Because they gave people too much knowledge on...'

'On what?' said Oona.

'Come, come and see', Eclipse urged. 'By the way, to make your chair go, tell it.'

Oona followed Eclipse up the shelves and shelves of books until they reached the big book at the top titled, *The Killer Plant*. Oona read the blurb, *Dear Reader, I must explain that there are people who wish to destroy the world with a killer plant.*

Eclipse explained, 'You know the hypo 3160s let us...'

'The what?' chimed in Oona.

'The robots, anyway, they let us through.'

'Yes,' Oona lifted her head as she spoke.

Then Eclipse said, 'It's because Aslan O'Brien, the prime minister, my father, left me to look after this tower. My sister, Eeka and Oleander have to look after other zones. Eeka has charge of the Garden of Silver and Oleander takes care of the Fountain of Youth, but don't worry about those. I, Eclipse O'Brien was given the job to look after the Tower of Mystery. Do you follow?'

'Yes, Sir', saluted Oona.

'Anyway, this book tells you how to grow a most terrible plant and if anyone steps within 100,000,000 kilometres of it, it squirts gunpowder and acid and destroys the world,' continued Eclipse, 'That's why books are banned,' smiled Eclipse.

'Banned!' exclaimed Oona, astounded. She loved books!

'Yeah, they were banned in case they contained any killer plant information,' said Eclipse.

'Were you not sad?' exclaimed Oona.

'No, I was in favour of it, you should have seen the havoc they caused,' lectured Eclipse.

'Where are all the books?' thought Oona.

'Here,' Eclipse read her thoughts.

Just at that moment, the walls started to flash and screech.

'Time, time, time, 20:30, time.'

Oona was taken aback, 'W, w, w, wh why are are the the the they'd, d, d doing th th this?'

'Bedtime,' smiled Eclipse.

Oona followed her down ten flights of steps and then saw two beds floating. Not thinking, Oona and Eclipse fell onto the beds.

Eclipse said, 'Light off' and immediately the lights turned off and they slept peacefully.

When Oona woke up, she waited to hear Kasha's screaming, but it never came.

She opened her eyes and saw Eclipse asleep on the other bed and remembered what had happened.

She leaned over and tapped Eclipse, 'Let's check on the book, Eclipse,' she said excitedly.

'Huh?' said Eclipse sleepily at first, then, 'Oh yes, we'd better.'

They both jumped out of bed and ran up the 35 flights of stairs to the grand stand.

'Noooooooo,' screamed Eclipse.

'The book is gone', gasped Oona.

'Right let's do this how we should', panicked Eclipse. Then she shouted, 'Finger print analyser'.

The wall opened and let out a small box with a camera-like lens.

Eclipse picked it up and moved it over the grand stand.

Then in a robotic voice it said, 'The finger prints belong to Allium Allemand who is a major criminal from France. He is 34 and lives at 13 Boating Street, Oxford, England.'

'Thanks Allie,' smiled Eclipse, then ordered, 'Desmond, come at once'.

Desmond, a robot with a red visor, strode up.

'Look after the house, order,' commanded Eclipse.

Desmond nodded and walked back.

Immediately, Oona and Eclipse ran out of the door, turned right, left and right again until they found number

13 Boating Street.

They crashed through the door and Oona said, 'Allium, come at once, it's your mother.'

'Andrea,' chimed in Eclipse.

Oona stood blankly staring, but Eclipse ran out of the room on to the street and up to a woman who, according to Allie the robot looked like Allium's mum. The lady was called Rosalinda and Eclipse explained her plan. Then off they ran, back to 13 Boating Street.

Back at number 13, Eclipse pulled Oona out of the way and Rosalinda checked they were safely under cover as talking teenagers.

Then she started, 'Allium, Allium, come at once, it's me Andrea,' hollered Rosalinda.

'Ahh, mum, what do you want to speak about?'

'Well, first you must come to the police station. I need help,' acted Rosalinda.

'Okay, okay', agreed Allium, he knew his mum was going on 80, but she had never asked this much of her child, it was strange. 'Can't we teleport, mum?' enquired Allium as they were about to go out of the door.

Rosalinda followed Allium down to the basement, walked through the big black machine and said poshly, 'Police station'. Within 12 seconds they had arrived.

Just then, Eclipse and Oona walked through the door.

'Yes!' thought relieved Rosalinda as Eclipse and Oona wandered through the door.

'Who?' questioned Allium.

'Witnesses,' explained Rosalinda calmly.

Next moment a straight capped, pale faced and weary eyed man looked up at them.

'A cat up a tree?' suggested the man. 'I am P. C. Robert, police chief, your matter?' said P. C Robert.

'Well,' started Rosalinda, 'The book The Killer Plant.'

'Yes', nodded P. C Robert.

'Well, it's been stolen'.

Allium gasped and backed away.

'Allium,' said Rosalinda sternly.

P. C Robert gasped, 'Any witnesses?'

'Yes, this is Eclipse O'Brien and Oona Tellick,' explained Rosalinda.

'And the culprit?' asked P. C Robert.

'He is right here', smiled Rosalinda. 'And Allium, I am not your mother, I am Rosalinda Kerfu'.

Allium was chained up and taken away.

Rosalinda, Eclipse and Oona smiled at one another, and then left.

Outside, Eclipse and Oona thanked Rosalinda as she left to walk down Mystery Lane.

Eclipse and Oona went back to Allium's house, picked up the book and replaced it, but when Oona returned to the tower, a completely different matter came to her head, how to get home. She saw the sky turn the orangeish-purple, then Eclipse broke her thoughts by suggesting, 'Wanna sleep outside?'

'Yeah!' exclaimed Oona, on her way to get home at last.

At 20:30 they went to bed in a tent on the moor and shortly fell asleep, but when Oona woke up she was in her moor!

She felt so happy because she knew the future was saved and she could enjoy the rest of her holiday on the Isle of Wight.

PARADISE

By Bella Evans
Year 4

CHAPTER 1

Amelia lay on her bed while her brother, Thomas, was cooking eggs and soldiers. Amelia could smell the lovely, delicious bread cooking so it forced her to leap out of bed and race down the steep stairs. Thomas was just opening the door with a smile on his pale face with a letter in his hand

Then he said, in a quick voice, 'I am going to fight a war!'

Then, immediately, Amelia's face turned happy to sad. Suddenly, she said in a quiet voice, 'But who is going to look after me?'

A long pause began.

Then Thomas said, still very excited, 'Do not fear, Amelia, I will be back at Christmas!'

'But, that's seven months away,' cried Amelia.

'Do not cry, Amelia. I have also told Aunty Hillary to look after you. You are going to have great fun with her.

Amelia was not so sure about this aunty coming round…

CHAPTER 2

Amelia was happy now because Thomas told her all about the fun times he had with Aunty Hillary (but I do not think they were true).

It was the day of the aunty coming round.

Suddenly, there was a loud knock on the door. My brother ran to the door and opened it. There stood a tall, stern looking lady. She had her black hair tied into a bun. Then Amelia noticed a large, hairy wart sticking out on the side of her cheek. She sniggered.

'Excuse me! What are you looking at? Go to the kitchen and think about your behaviour! NOW! Amelia stomped off to the kitchen and sat down on a chair feeling frustrated.

About 15 minutes later, the Aunty burst into the kitchen, 'Go and pack your bags.'

Amelia rushed before the lady would change her mind, but she was too early.

'STOP, what do you say to me?'

Amelia said sorry in a quiet, sorry voice.

'Pardon?' said the lady.

'Sorry.'

'That's better. Now go.'

Amelia started to pack her bag, toothbrush, brush, teddy, pyjamas, clothes and diary.

Anything else? I think that is all she said to herself.

CHAPTER 3

Amelia kissed her brother on the cheek.

'Bye,' she said, as a tear ran down Amelia's face.

Thomas walked off and disappeared into the house.

Amelia was already in the car.

'Now *he* is gone,' the Aunty said, 'Do not touch my silk seats! Get off them immediately!'

Amelia did not know what to say. Aunty started the car. Suddenly, there was a loud roar from the engine of the car. Amelia felt a shiver run down her spine. Each minute seemed like an hour. Then Amelia looked through the window. It was starting to rain because the windows were steamed up. She held up her finger and drew a love heart (forgetting about the Aunty), but the Aunty was watching Amelia very closely.

CHAPTER 4

Later on that evening, Amelia lay on her new bed. She peered around the room. She could see the blackout curtain and the dusty shelves with old books. There was also a tatty chair and a chest of drawers (to put her clothes in) and a brightly coloured eiderdown on the top of the bed. Amelia sat up and was swinging her legs.

'Ouch!' said Amelia. She had banged her leg on something hard.

'*What is that?*' she thought, curiously.

She poked her head round. Then she saw a large dusty chest. She pulled it out. She opened it apprehensively and saw a colourful train underneath a pile of music sheets. She took out the train and held it in her hand, the metal felt cold on her skin.

'Oh, I would love to be on a train going away from this horrible house.'

Then she felt suddenly very tired. She fell into a deep, deep sleep. When she woke she could feel the motion of a train. When she looked around she could not believe her eyes! There were lots of people chattering and then a girl with blonde hair tied into plaits sat next to her.

Amelia said, in a confused voice, 'Where am I?'

'Don't you know? We are on the train to Paradise.'

'Where is that?' said Amelia.

'Hmmm, it is hard to explain because it is in the future. Why don't you come with me?'

'Excuse me, but what is your name?' said Amelia.

'It is Sarah,' she replied.

'Well, nice to meet you, Sarah.'

CHAPTER 5

Suddenly, the train stopped.

A short man stood and announced, 'If you want to go to Paradise, come this way immediately!'

Amelia followed Sarah. Then they stepped off the train and Amelia had an overwhelming feeling of happiness. There was a flowing, glistening waterfall, a swirling mist, beautiful flowers and a sunset.

'Come on then,' said Sarah. 'Let's go to the cake shop.'

The cake shop had delightful cakes. Some sponge, some chocolate cake, some with lots of decorations on them. Amelia first looked at the fruit cake with lots of marzipan shaped like flowers on the cake. Amelia held out her penny politely to the lady behind the delicious cakes.

'Which one would you like?' said the lady.

'That one, please,' said Amelia.

'There you go then.'

Sarah whispered in Amelia's ear, 'You do not pay for anything in Paradise.'

CHAPTER 6

Amelia and Sarah were at a time travel museum. They were at a past machine.

Sarah said, 'You can wish to anywhere you want to in the past and change it.'

Amelia already had an idea… her parents sadly died in World War I (killed by a bomb) but she could travel back in time and warn them not to go outside when the bombs were being released. She asked Sarah how to make her dream come true.

Sarah said, 'Just press that big, red button, close your eyes and imagine you are there and stopping that person from the dilemma or changing that moment.'

Amelia put both hands on the button without putting any pressure on the button.

She whispered in her mother and father's ear, 'Do not go outside.' And Amelia kept on repeating that speech in their ears.

The parents agreed on staying in the house and not even looking outside.

Suddenly, Amelia opened her eyes…

CHAPTER 7

Sarah said, urgently, 'Quickly, hurry, I know the train is leaving in another 5 minutes.'

'Oh, we better hurry then,' said Amelia.

The two girls ran to the train quicker than a flash.

The man announced, 'Sit down, and make yourselves comfortable. We are leaving *now*!

'So, how do I make myself vanish back home?' asked Amelia.

'That is easy. Just fall asleep and think about where you live,' replied Sarah.

Amelia fell asleep and thought about the dusty shelves, the blackout curtains, and the best of them all the toy train.

Then Amelia got awoken by a loud knock on the door. She opened her eyes and gazed around dreamily, but this was not her Aunties house. This was her old house! Amelia's memory began to remember. This was her room before the bomb fell!

She ran down the stairs confused.

'Mum, you are alive!' She gave her a big cuddle.

'What is all the fuss about?' said Mum.

'Where is Dad?'

'He is in the garden?'

Amelia rushed outside, 'Dad, you are alive too!'

Amelia closed her eyes and whispered, '*Thank you, Paradise.*'

TIME TRAVEL

By Abbie Hartley
Year 4

One day in the shops was a time travel hat that takes you back in time.

One day, when I was walking past the shop, I decided to buy the hat.

A couple of days later, I tried the hat on. And I could not believe my eyes.

It took me back in time to the Tudor times. But, it was very unusual. All of the Tudor's were all executing their enemies and actually frying people in boiling hot water. I was absolutely horrified. So, just then I felt something clip on both of my hands. I was getting my head chopped off by the Tudors.

I took my hat off and very quickly I was back in my house getting a cup of tea for my Mum and Dad. And I was reading my books and magazines. And then the kettle went off, so I went to get the cups out and pour the tea into the cups.

I gave them the cup of tea and I went up the stairs and had another time travel. But, in that time travel it was so different. I went back into the Victorian time. I was very confused because I was wearing a big puppy dress. And all of the other people was to. But, of course the boys weren't. They were wearing a suit with a tie and some curly wigs. But, some was falling off and that was scaring me somehow. So, you know what I did? I took my hat off and I was back at my house reading my book and magazine.

And that was the time travelling story…

THE TIME TRAVELLING TV

By Grace Roberts
Year 4

'I wish it would stop snowing,' Millie groaned, throwing the last magazine back on the pile, and then glancing towards the window at her brother playing in the snow.

'Well, you could go and play in the snow, like your brother,' her mother replied.

It was the Christmas holidays and Millie was at her grandma's house. It had a rose garden, a river, a green house, a pond, a nursery, an orchard and even a swimming pool!

But, Millie would not go out because she hated the snow!

Millie had done everything to stop the boredom. She had read all the magazines, played all the board games, and watched all the boring channels on her grandmother's ancient TV. Millie had always wondered if there was something different to her grandmother's TV than her one at home. Yes, of course it was older, but something about the channels and what times they were filmed, made Millie thought of Victorian times. But, she wasn't sure if they had cameras back then, and it bothered her the way the TV fuzzed around as if lots of tiny flies were trapped inside.

Millie's grandmother walked into the room.

'Why aren't you outside, Millie?' her grandmother asked, with a puzzled expression on her face.

'Millie hated the snow,' Millie's mother replied, looking at Millie in a stern way.

'Well Millie, why don't I tell you a story?' her grandmother asked.

'Okay, said Mille.'

Well, have you heard the legend of the secret gateway?' her grandmother said, slowly thinking.

'No,' said Millie, 'tell me.'

'Well, it was a long time ago, about a hundred years from now. It is to be said that in a secret garden there is a secret gateway leading to places unknown of.' Her grandmother stopped for a breath, and then thought very hard.

'Go on, tell me more,' said Millie, intrigued with her grandmother's story.

'Well, it is also to be said that at the end of the secret gateway is a mine, and if you go further down the mine there is a slide all the way to an unknown world.'

'Have you ever been to the unknown world,' Millie asked.

'No, never,' said her grandmother. 'It probably isn't even in my garden, Millie. There are lots of gardens in England, Millie.' Millie's grandmother sighed, 'Well, we can't be sitting around all day. I'm going to the shops. Who's coming?'

They all went to the shops in the car to buy some warm soup for tea. After they had tea it was bedtime. Millie trudged up the stairs to her cosy bed, but she could not stop thinking about the secret gateway. Finally, she made up her mind to try and find the gateway the next day.

*

The next day after breakfast, Millie went straight downstairs and straight into the garden. She looked for the secret gateway all morning, but had no sign of it. Finally, she gave up. On her way walking back to the house, she noticed an old gate saying *mine*. Millie was so excited she rushed down to it to find what she was looking for...

The gate was old and dusty, but when Millie wiped some of the dust off with her mitten she realised that the gate was very strange. It had strange markings of elves and leaves, and had an ivy creeper up one side. The gate was locked, but Millie realised a small hole that hadn't been there before. The hole was getting bigger and bigger...

Millie felt a wind around her, whipping her up and sending her straight through the hole, and then there was nothing left of Millie except two footprints in the snow.

Millie felt nervous and excited at the same time. All she could see were rainbow colours hovering above a pool of water. She felt butterflies in her stomach and she wondered if it was all a dream. Although Millie felt nervous this was so much better than being bored indoors.

Slowly, Millie's eyes could see a huge TV screen all around her. It looked just like one of the TV shows off of her grandma's old TV with the same fuzzy motion. Suddenly, Millie felt that wind around her, but this time it was sending her right at the TV screen. Millie was scared she would hit it so she closed her eyes. She suddenly felt a whoosh and found herself inside the television, and she was standing in a lane.

A small girl suddenly skipped up to her and said, 'Do you have a farthing I could borrow?'

Millie did not know what a farthing was, but she had seen one in her History book. Millie felt absentmindedly in her dress pocket and to her surprise she found a small coin.

'Ah, just what a need!' exclaimed the girl, reaching out for the coin.

'Is this a farthing?' Millie asked.

The small girl nodded, and then Millie handed the coin over and watched the girl skip off down the lane.

Millie wondered down the lane and saw lots of little cottages. People were staring at her. She wondered if they were looking at her clothes, as she felt very out of place in her pink snow jacket and salopettes. Everyone was wearing stripped frocks and top hats. They all looked very grand. Millie was getting hungry.

Finally, a kind, old woman, who looked very much like her own grandmother, came out of her house and said to Millie, 'You should be inside by now. Are you hungry?'

Millie nodded.

The old lady led Millie by her hand into her cosy, little cottage. The cottage had lovely floral wallpaper with flowers on every window sill. But, Millie thought it was rather small.

The old lady read her mind. 'I know the cottage is

small, but it's just about big enough for me. Sit yourself down at the table and I'll fetch you some warm soup,' said the old woman, as she wondered to the kitchen.

The soup was delicious, but after a while Millie began to feel tired.

'Go upstairs and rest,' the old lady said.

Millie did just that.

The bed was really comfortable and soon she was fast asleep.

*

The next morning Millie woke up to find herself in her own cosy bed at her grandmother's house.

She rushed downstairs to find her Grandma sitting at the table fiddling with her old TV, 'Oh! Silly television, it's broken,' she said.

Millie told her about her adventure.

'What a dream you had, Millie,' her grandma said with a twinkle in her eye.

THE MAGIC GUINEA PIGS

By Erin Tellick
Year 4

One sunny Saturday, there was a girl called Laura who was off to the local, rodent rescue.

She was walking up the cobble, stone path when she noticed a sign for charity.

It read *MR TWIDDLE'S RODENT RESCUE.*

She knocked on the door and heard a deep, croaky voice inviting her to come in.

Inside, Laura was confronted by a room filled with china plates and a lovely, warm, spicy smell. It wasn't quite what Laura had been expecting. All of a sudden, Laura realised there was an old man sitting in a wooden rocking chair, stroking a silky, white rabbit. He was wearing half-moon spectacles and a tapestry pattern, velvet gown. He had scruffy, grey hair and a long, grey beard.

Laura asked if she could visit the guinea pigs.

He led her down a grassy path. Ahead, she could see a small, old wooden barn. Inside there were 10 to 12 pens dividing up the barn. Each pen housed 2 to 3 rabbits or guinea pigs.

Laura was enchanted by one particular guinea pig. He had hazel eye and a pink, snuffle nose which seemed to never stop twitching, and he had long, soft fur which stuck out in black, white and brown tuffs.

She asked, 'Can I hold him?'

Mr Twiddle said, 'Only if you are careful. This guinea pig is special.'

He undid the latch, ushered Laura to a stall and put him on her lap. He felt very soft and silky.

'He does not have a name yet. You could name him if you like?'

'Could I call him Wilfred?'

'Yes, if you like. Have you ever had a guinea pig before?'

'Yes, I've got an Abersynian called Dandelion Dave, but I call him Dandy for short.'

In the hour that Laura spent stroking Wilfred and chatting to Mr Twiddle time seemed to stand still.

Just as Laura was about to ask if she could re-home Wilfred, Mr Twiddle got there first and said, 'So, you're really serious? You want to keep him then? Do your parents know you're here?'

'Yes,' replied Laura, 'they're waiting in the car outside. In fact, I had better go. They will be wondering why I'm taking so long.'

'Don't worry. I'm sure it will be fine.'

She ran back to the car and hurried her parents back up to the path to Mr Twiddle.

*

Half an hour later, Laura was back home with Wilfred, showing him to Dandelion Dave. The two guinea pigs were sniffing each other through the bars, squeaking little chirrupy sounds to each other.

'Mum, I think they're friends already. I'm going to put them together.'

'Okay Laura, but don't leave them alone yet.'

'Yes, Mum, I know!'

Laura put both guinea pigs into the pen in her bedroom and sat to watch. They snuffled each other, and then got on with the important job of eating.

*

A little while later, Laura's mum called her down to lunch. Laura gave both one last stroke and rubbed them behind their ears. Just as Laura rubbed Wilfred behind his ear an amazing thing happened. The room started to spin with swirling, purple mist. When the mist cleared, Laura was sitting in a rainforest clearing and in the distance she could see an Aztec Pyramid reaching up to the sky. A little confused, but very interested, Laura walked towards the pyramid.

Into view now came an Aztec Temple, and the roof was held up by golden columns at each side of the entrance. Laura entered the temple and inside she discovered a large, central courtyard with terraced seating all around. There were guards posted at each side of the courtyard entrance, wearing gold and feathered head dresses and colour, patterned tunics.

There were crowds of cheering Aztecs filling the terraced seating and, in the courtyard, athletic looking men were playing a strange game, a bit like basketball. There was a fixed hoop on one wall, very high up, and the players were in two teams, each trying to score a goal by throwing a heavy, leather ball through the hoop.

Just then, a tiny Chihuahua trotted up to Laura and

sniffed her ankle. Laura went down to stroke the tiny, little dog and as she tickled him behind his ears Laura found herself surrounded by a swirling, purple mist.

When it cleared Laura was sitting back in her bedroom on the floor. Laura rushed to the bathroom to wash her hands and hurried to the kitchen for lunch.

'You were quick,' said Laura's mum.

'Oh, yeah, I'm quite hungry,' said Laura, feeling a little surprised, as it felt like ages ago that she had heard her mum calling.

He really is special, Mr Twiddle was right...

LAZY MAZY'S REVENGE

By Elsa Wester

Year 4 JOINT WINNER

It was a hot, sunny day in town. Meanwhile, a few miles away in a hut in the wood secret plotting was going on, and I don't mean vegetable plotting.

That night it was very misty and the late traffic was going by when suddenly there was a screeching of tires and bright lights flew round the corner. The car stopped abruptly in the front of the science museum. A woman in a black jumpsuit jumped out, and run to the front the bank with a gun in her hand. She was in and out quickly. As she left she had a strange contraption in her hand.

Once in the car, she shrieked, 'Finally, my revenge on that mean town'

But at the town which she had cursed they slept soundly. As they slept a foggy, mysterious green glow went around the town and without warning the town folk disappeared!

Where had the people gone was the question on many people's lips. Some thought that they had been taken ransom; others thought they had been abducted by aliens. The police were swarming everywhere looking in every nook and cranny of the place. The fact the town's folk had disappeared was the only clear clue! People were about to hear it all over the world! But, as for the robbery, people just weren't hearing as much as they should have heard about it.

Know I will tell you where the town's people went.

Why they were there, and who the woman was and how she linked in?

Well, it all started two months ago, and to cut a long story short they dropped a bee's hive on girls head and they did it because she was too lazy and this girl was called Mazy and guess who stole the object which was a time machine.

Well, onto what happened to the town folk, bearing in mind they didn't know that a time machine had been stolen. Well, what had happened was they had gone to sleep normally and well this is a town folk's account of what had happened

*

Dear Diary

19 June 2013

Yesterday I went to sleep normally but when I woke up, I thought I was having a nightmare because there was a grubby faced person staring down at me with a mixture of confusion, annoyance, horror and determination on his

face.

'Who are you?' we both asked at the same time.

He had an Egyptian accent, 'Are you a spy and are any of them spies?'

'No,' I answered quickly. I didn't want this person, my enemy whoever he was, 'Excuse me, but where am I?'

'You don't know where you are? Well, this is Egypt of course. The place of dreams, the never ending kingdom'

'You can't be serious, is the year near 300bc?'

'Yes, of course'

And with that I blacked out.

When I woke, I could hear moans and groans all around me. I had been thinking it all over had gone insane? I mean unless I'm part of some crazy joke this is impossible! But, supposing that I had somehow travelled back in time. Hadn't I heard on the telly that a time machine had been invented and hadn't it been proven that the time machine worked?

I wondered if the time machine had been stolen, but who would hate the town that much? It could be that horrid boy we exiled because he made Mr Nancy faint, no he knew why we'd done it. Wait, how could I have been so blind? Wouldn't that infernal girl, Mazy, have the motivation to do such a thing and I'm sure she's not lazy anymore. Hmmm, yes, I'm sure she'd do it. I'm definitely right, how are we going to get ourselves back?

*

Little did this town's person know that she was spot on and a rescue plan was already in action…?

Because a great inspector had been studying the cases

of the robbery having an instinct that they were connected. He had almost given up, when he had stumbled upon something interesting. Apparently, the town was rather badly known for dropping a bee's hive on a girl called Mazy's head, and hadn't the person who had stolen the time machine yelled, *'Finally, my revenge on that mean little town.'*

When he had found this, he had immediately telephoned the chief inspector who had nearly choked on his jam donut. 'Yes' he spluttered, ejecting his jam donut onto his work, 'I will have your theory checked and we will check out this Mazy character.' His five chins were wobbling in excitement and his honey, blond hair was dripping with sweat (not that there was much hair).

When they checked it out, they found he was right and well this is an inspector's report of the raid on Mazy's house

*

Barnsley's report on the raid on Mazy's house

21 June 2013

We were sliding along the road as usual on a raid. When we got to the suspect's house we got out all ready, when suddenly Jennifer fainted. We all reacted and immediately saw that she had been hit with a tranquilizer dart. We all got out are shields and Barry reported what had happened.

We slowly came up the front gate. We smashed the door down and then ran upstairs. I could hear the two others clashing around down stairs. I came to a bedroom. I could see a strange purple glow inside.

I got my gun out and slowly edged inside.

There was the time machine!

That detective was a genius, but I had not been careful enough, because I turned round on instinct just in time to dodge away from the bullet which was rocketing towards me, it missed me by a millimetre.

I ran down the hall in hot pursuit of a small figure which was obviously Mazy.

I was shouting for back up, but unluckily, the dufoses Barry and bob were gorging themselves on sweets and chocolate they had found in the pantry. But, luckily Jennifer had woken up (the saviour), heard my urgent pleas for help and caught the criminal.

She had stuffed her in the back.

After shouting at Barry and Bob and thanking Jennifer warmly, I proceeded to checking on the criminal and driving the criminal to HQ.

When Mazy got to HQ, she was questioned and found guilty and that is how a rescue plan was put into action but what had the towns' people been thinking at the time?

*

Dear Diary

20 June 2013

Nothing exciting happened except for when I met up with the rest of the townspeople and when a guard came in saying that in three days hence we were to be seen before Queen Cleopatra.

*

Dear Diary

23 June 2013

Today we were herded along the streets like sheep (I've never fully appreciated how horrible it is) with the Egyptians staring at us like we were from another planet.

Eventually, after what seemed like hours of walking, but it was probably just ten minutes, we reached the palace. There were probably a 1000 steps going up and up as far as the eye could see. It was hard to deny the splendour of the building. No, it was a monument we were marched up.

The servants here must have a good strong legs, I wouldn't last an hour.

At the top of the stairs, when we finally got there, was a chamber filled with vases of exotic flowers in them. The chamber was open air, and lying under the couch that was embodied with all sorts of weird and wonderful patterns.

Well, under it was a leopard. The leopard was beautiful, with eyes that looked like turquoise pools and razor sharp teeth which were like daggers. But none of this out shone the woman sitting on the couch. She had inky black hair, eyeliner all around her eyes, which where hazel green and burning with undisguised curiosity.

Then she spoke. Her voice was high and piercing, yet it was welcoming at the same time, 'Who are you?' she asked.

(The mayor had goo eyes)

'We are from England,' I said; because the mayor was unable to actual speak.

'Where is England, what is England?' Cleopatra rushed on.

'Well, I will tell you, but all of the guards and servants can't come in or be in here and they definitely can't hear.'

Cleopatra considered, and then waved her hand and all the servants and guards went away, 'Now, tell me your story,' she demanded.

I started at the beginning, Cleopatra was a good listener.

At the end, she asked, 'And the future of Egypt?'

Her question was interrupted by a zinging sound and suddenly tons of people were standing in front of us grinning broadly.

'It's time we took you home,' they said.

'And the future of Egypt?' Cleopatra yelled.

'Not much in it, Mark Anthony or Octavian, but a bit of advice burn with your treasure, make sure you do it!'

Then suddenly my vision was full of blue spirals and then we were home!

In the end, I wrote a book about what had happened, collecting all the information I could find, and this is the finished work!

SHELBY AND THE PINK BOOTS

By Jessica Dixon
Year 5

One sunny day, Shelby was enjoying her summer holidays at home.

Suddenly, her mum and dad came in and said, 'Do you want to come to the shops with us?'

Shelby replied, 'Okay, yes. That would be nice.'

She got her shoes and coat on and got in the car ready to go shopping.

After walking around the shops for a while, she came across her favourite shoe shop and went inside. When inside she could not find anything she liked, but just at that moment she saw a large poster saying, NEW, NEW, NEW PINK BOOTS.

Shelby could not find these pink boots, so she went to go and ask the assistant where they were.

The assistant said, 'Oh, we have not got them yet. I will go and get you a pair from the back.'

When she came back with the boots, Shelby could not wait to try them on. They fitted perfectly. Shelby did not know that the boots she had put on were magic, and they would send her on an adventure into the future, and that's what they did.

Shelby found herself in the same shoe shop, but now she was in the future. Shelby looked around and saw a pair of boots that had wings on the side. She asked the assistant what the wings were for, and she said they make you fly.

Shelby did not hesitate, and said, 'I will have a pair. But, how much are they?'

'They are 50 sweet wrappers,' said the assistant.

Shelby was puzzled and put her hand in her pocket, and was about to say, *all I have is* when she realised that her money had changed into sweet wrappers. She took them out of her pocket and had just enough wrappers to pay for the shoes.

She was so excited that she put them on straight away and flew out of the shop and into the sky. Only to see that this way the way everybody was travelling around.

From the air, she could see all over the town. She looked down and she saw a long queue of people waiting to go underground, so she flew down with her flying shoes to find out why.

When she got there she saw a pathway going underground.

When she went in she found it was an underground ride. It took you around a maze of 10 caves, and in each cave you had to collect a golden ball. If you successfully collected all 10 golden balls you were given a token that you could use for anything you wanted.

Shelby decided that she wanted to have a go, but when she arrived at the first cave and went into it she found herself back in her own time.

She was in the shoe shop, and the shop assistant said, 'Are you going to buy the pink books now?'

Shelby and her Mum said, 'Yes,' at the same time.

The Ancient Temple

By Sophie Hartley
Year 5

Once upon a time, in Ancient Greece, there was a father and his two daughters called Sofia and Abigail. They were polite, pretty, sweet and kind. Sofia had hair as long as an elephant's trunk, it was ginger and soft. She also had blue eyes, red rosy cheeks, and a short green pleated dress, with matching bows for her long plaits. Therefore, Abigail was mostly exactly the same, except the fact that she had blonde plaits and her bows and dress were orange.

The girls' dad realised one day that after all of this time the girls had been helping and working around the villa to keep it neat and tidy. He had not yet repaid the girls for all of their help.

So one night, Pheilius (dad/father) was up all night wondering what he could do.

Then, as quick as a flash, he thought of something, something extravagant, ginormous, humungous (if that is what you would call it). So he jumped up from his sofa bed and went outside in the pouring rain and the thunder and lightning to get started on his new project.

At precisely 9:00 a.m. in the morning the girls wondered where their father had been, as he told them that he had to do some emergency jobs for his boss.

'Abigail, Abigail, come over here. Look!' exclaimed Sofia, as surprised as can be. 'Look, it's, it's – a – a – a...'

'A TEMPLE,' shrieked Abigail. 'Well, what are you waiting for Ab's? Let's go!'

As the girls were indeed very excited, they started to see something that was getting closer and closer by the second.

The girls rushed out to see who or what it was.

It was their father ... but, he was with someone else, he was with the paramedic and two horses. One of the horses was brown and the other was a dapple, grey horse, but also, strangely enough, they BOTH had saddles on them. All of them came in, even the horses!

The ambulance explained that he had been struck by lightning but was still okay.

The next day, Pheilius was much better and let the girls go out and play in the temple and with the horses.

As far as I know, the temple is still up and in tip top condition today.

THE ADVENTURES OF EINSTEIN'S CATS

By Beatrice Kirkby

Year 5 WINNER

The adventure began with Einstein's cats called Mia-ow and Hans. Mia-ow likes to sleep, drink milk and play with Einstein's children. Hans likes catching mice, climbing trees and altogether being very mischievous.

One day, when the children had gone to school and Einstein had gone to work, Mia-ow said, 'I'm bored.'

Hans replied, 'Let's go and explore.'

So off they went.

After a while, they came across a large wicker chair. It reminded them of their cat basket, on the chair had light and buttons around it.

They both felt tired by now and decided to sit on the chair and rest.

Hans pressed on of the buttons as he climbed in the chair and, all of a sudden, all the lights starting flashing and whoosh! They began to fly through the air and out of the open window and up through the clouds.

They both stared at each other in horror.

They saw a note on the chair saying, BROKEN, IN NEED OF REPAIR – EINSTEIN'S TIME MACHINE.

Suddenly, they landed and felt a bit confused because they were in the middle of triangle shapes made of sand.

They both realised the time machine had taken them back to the Egyptian times.

They both crept inside a Pyramid and they saw Cleopatra lying in her tomb.

Then they heard a loud noise.

The Pyramid was being closed up by a big stone.

'Quick,' said Hans, 'or we will be buried alive with Cleopatra.'

Mia-ow and Hans quickly ran and jumped back onto the time machine.

This time Mia-ow pressed a button.

They landed with a thud! This time they had landed at the top of a very large tree. They both climbed down and saw a sign saying, HARD WORKING CATS WANTED FOR NEW BROOMSTICK (Milk, fish and anything you want in return).

They decided to follow it.

A few minutes later, they arrived at a cottage and knocked on the door.

The door opened and an old lady said, 'Come in. Would you like to be my cats?'

Mia-ow and Hans said, 'Yes, we would.'

They were half way through their cream when someone knocked on the door.

They heard a loud voice say, 'We have come to take you away. We think you are a witch and we will have the cats too.'

Quickly, Mia-ow and Hans ran and climbed back up

the tree and got back up onto the time machine.

Whoosh!

Off they went, this time going to Ten Downing Street.

Eventually, Mia-ow and Hans landed in Ten Downing Street. They walked up to the big, black door.

Unfortunately, there were two big, brown dogs guarding the door.

Mia-ow and Hans were afraid.

The door opened and Mia-ow and Hans quickly ran in and down a long corridor.

They ran into a room and saw David Cameron speaking to a crowd of people. He said, 'This is top secret. I am going to ban cats as I am allergic to them.'

Hans said, 'We better get out Mia-ow. Quick!'

They both ran back to the time machine and whoooosh! They both pressed a button and this time they were up to 10,000 years in the future.

Magically, they landed in a strange world, where all cats had time machines and were a lot more intelligent.

They decided to borrow a time machine and go home.

Amazingly, the time machine was exactly like the one they had found in Einstein's office…

TIME SLIP STORIES

By Year 6

These "Time Slip Stories" were written by year 6 pupils a few weeks before their SATs. We decided to include them to give you a flavour of the kind of work children do at the upper end of primary school.

The children were given 55 minutes under exam conditions to produce a narrative story with an element of time travel.

They were told to include a main character, a best friend or relative, and a friend from the past.

This is what some of them wrote…

the tree and got back up onto the time machine.

Whoosh!

Off they went, this time going to Ten Downing Street.

Eventually, Mia-ow and Hans landed in Ten Downing Street. They walked up to the big, black door.

Unfortunately, there were two big, brown dogs guarding the door.

Mia-ow and Hans were afraid.

The door opened and Mia-ow and Hans quickly ran in and down a long corridor.

They ran into a room and saw David Cameron speaking to a crowd of people. He said, 'This is top secret. I am going to ban cats as I am allergic to them.'

Hans said, 'We better get out Mia-ow. Quick!'

They both ran back to the time machine and whoooosh! They both pressed a button and this time they were up to 10,000 years in the future.

Magically, they landed in a strange world, where all cats had time machines and were a lot more intelligent.

They decided to borrow a time machine and go home.

Amazingly, the time machine was exactly like the one they had found in Einstein's office…

TIME SLIP STORIES

By Year 6

These "Time Slip Stories" were written by year 6 pupils a few weeks before their SATs. We decided to include them to give you a flavour of the kind of work children do at the upper end of primary school.

The children were given 55 minutes under exam conditions to produce a narrative story with an element of time travel.

They were told to include a main character, a best friend or relative, and a friend from the past.

This is what some of them wrote…

By Lily Ainslie

"Ahhh, this is the life," sighed Chloe, as she lay back and relaxed under the scorching Greek sun. This was by far the best holiday ever.

She thought of her friends back home, "Hmmm, they are probably doing maths now."

"Come on, Chloe. The battle re-enactments start at twelve o'clock and we don't want to be late!" called Mum.

Chloe rolled off her sun lounger, and fell onto the towel with a muffled thud. Why couldn't she just stay and sunbathe all day? She hated going to museums.

Before she knew it, she was watching the Athenian warriors defending their city from the invading Spartans. She wandered around the spectator arena, and then she noticed a door marked 'Actors only.' Well, it wouldn't hurt to just have a little peep, would it?

She gave the heavy door an almighty shove and it creaked open. The interior looked rather like the changing rooms at her local swimming pool, apart from the lack of a sodden floor.

The first thing that caught her eye was an Athenian warriors' garment. It looked as though it was for a small adult, about her size…

"Well, seeing as no-one is using it, why not give it a try," she said aloud to herself.

It was a little on the big size but it still looked good.

Just then, a man came in the door that she had just entered through. As he began to make his way towards her the room seemed to spin around and around.

As Chloe tried to sit down she realised that the bench behind her had vanished! A dense mist engulfed her, and when it cleared she was in the same room. Same size, shape and stone – but the furniture was completely different. To her left was a rack of spears and shields, and to her right was a whole shelf filled with helmets. They were identical except for the size.

Suddenly, about fifteen men burst into the room, all dressed the same as her.

Above the cacophony of noise, she could make out people yelling, "Quickly, quickly, arm yourselves, the Spartans are attacking!"

Chloe's first thought was that she was caught in yet another re-enactment. But, then again, she thought, maybe being in a re-enactment would be more exciting than watching it...

As quick as a flash, she grabbed a shield, with a Griffin on it, selected the best fitting helmet and yanked a spear from the rack. The disturbing thing was the spear looked extremely authentic, as did the shield. As she raced outside, all of the people were dressed like real Athenians, and to her surprise, the actors were running towards the city walls! Before she had time to consider the impossibility of her situation, a man with a ridiculous hairy thing coming out of his head gear beckoned Chloe to put her helmet on.

As she did so, the dizzy feeling came on again and the familiar mist engulfed her for the last time. When the mist cleared, the man was still running towards her, but he looked as though he had gained about an inch in the twenty five minutes that Chloe had spent in that strange place.

When at last he reached her, she recognised him immediately. "Dad!" she exclaimed.

"What on earth are you doing in here, Chloe?!"

"Oh, it's a long story, I can assure you," Chloe laughed.

"Well, let's get you out of these clothes, shall we?" smiled Dad.

"Okay, but I don't think I'll be wearing these again anytime soon," smiled Chloe back.

By Jacob Chapman

"Okay, I'm on my way," Dan talked into his mobile phone to his friend, Sarah, who was meeting him at the History Museum to find out extra information for their project on World War II (it was only five minutes up the road from where Dan lived, so it wouldn't take long).

When he arrived at the museum, Sarah was waiting outside the museum.

"Come on slowcoach, I've been waiting here for about five minutes," Sarah joked.

"No, you said one, it's five to one now!" Dan exclaimed. "So, in my books, I'm pretty early."

"Fair point. Anyway, shall we go in?"

Dan nodded in agreement whilst they walked in the museum.

Once they were in the main hall, something caught Dan's eye. "Look, Sarah, over there in the World War II exhibit. There's something really cool."

Sarah followed Dan as he dashed off towards the exhibit. Once Sarah got here she knew that Dan's excitement wasn't for nothing.

There, what looked like was genuine, was a gas mask.

"Wow, the door is even open," Sarah said, in amazement.

"Go on, try it on," Dan urged Sarah.

"No, you're the brave one," Sarah answered.

"Fine, I won't wimp out like you," Dan tormented.

Sarah stuck her tongue out at Dan whilst he was putting the mask on.

"Ah, well, you really look like a person from the…"

Sarah faded out whilst Dan's head filled with sparkles and banging in his ears.

He was unconscious.

When Dan woke up, he realised that he fainted whilst trying the gas mask on at the museum. Except that, he wasn't at the museum anymore. Instead, he was in an empty street filled with sirens screaming at his ears.

"Hey, what are you doing out here? Can't you hear the sirens?"

Dan was so dazed he didn't know what to do.

Finally, what looked like an old fashioned policeman, grabbed Dan beneath his arms and carried him to what appeared to be a safe looking house.

Once he was there, he saw a middle aged lady crumpled on the floor under a huge metal table.

"Excuse me, are you okay?" Dan said, anxiously.

"Yes, I'm just taking cover, and you should be too."

But, before he could answer, another set of sirens came on.

Then the old fashioned policeman appeared again. "Come on, you two, get your gas masks on," he shouted, whilst giving both of them a gas mask each.

Once he got it on, he felt dizzy and disorientated like he had before. He fell to the floor.

When he came around again, he heard someone saying

something to him.

It was Sarah. She was finishing her sentence, what she started before Dan fainted.

"Sarah," Dan shouted, relieved whilst pulling the gas mask off viciously.

"Dan, you look pale. Do you want to go back?"

"Yes, please. I've had enough for one day." Dan smiled.

By Oliver Goodall

"How boring are the Egyptians?" Josh mumbled to himself.

He had decided to visit the history museum to find out some information for his history project. His friend, who was called Jake, had also had the same idea as him.

"Come on, try it on!" Jake urged, gesturing to the Egyptian robes on display.

As soon as the tour guide had disappeared round the corner, Josh lingered for the robes.

"Ha, ha, ha," Jake laughed, "you look…"

Suddenly, the earth began to spin vigorously and Josh's head slumped onto a sandy surface.

His eyes flickered open to see the open sky and the glaring sunlight. How could this be? It was raining just a minute ago. He could taste all of the sand in his mouth and a huge pyramid loomed over him. The hairs stood up on the back of his neck as he realised where he was. The endless, vast sand dunes behind him were being blown onto his bare legs.

An iron grip suddenly dragged the poor boy back over to the pyramid.

"Why are you not doing your job?" the stranger's voice boomed.

Josh was dripping with sweat under the intense heat from the sun. He tried to protest that he was not supposed to be there. Despite his greatest efforts, he was shoved towards the grand inscriptions inscribed on the pyramid and his robe was yanked off him.

Josh had to admire the work that had been done. Sneakily, as soon as no one was looking, he snuck away to the entrance, dived through the door and stood still, gobsmacked of his surroundings.

"How on earth am I going to get that robe back?" The young lad questioned himself. He saw numerous footprints leading through a stone archway and decided to follow him. He was stopped in his tracks as he sprinted into the back of someone.

As quick as a flash, he was gone, only leaving a cloud of sand. There was a row of robes which were being sorted that people were being given to wear.

He ran back outside the pyramid, scuttled up to the side of it and stopped abruptly when he came to the top.

He had researched lots of information about pyramids. If you removed the right brick at the top it would weaken the whole structure. With all of his might, he removed the top brick and the whole building shook violently. He leaped back down the side of the building just soon enough. Crash! Bricks tumbled down the edge and a swarm of people came bursting through the front.

Creeping silently, Josh snuck to where the costumes were. He leapt at the last remaining one and he waited to see his friend, Jake, again.

It never happened. He almost cried out in desperation.

A stranger stopped in front of him. "What do you think you are doing?" he demanded.

"I fear that this is unsafe to wear," Josh made up, gesturing to the robe.

"The last person who wore it never came back. It would be much safer to wear this one." He grumbled and unwillingly handed it over.

He shook until Jake came back into view.

"... very strange is that thing." Jake finished, as if nothing had happened.

"Come on, let's hear how the best pyramid ever built was destroyed – just by one boy!" Jake suggested excitedly.

Josh could barely contain himself as he blurted out the story to Jake. He suddenly walks off in disgust at his friend.

"I will do the best history project ever!" Josh said excitedly to the lady at the front desk as he walked off jollily back home.

By Ben Jennings

"Eeew!" said Harry, with a horrified expression on his face. "Who uses sponges on sticks for toilet tissue?"

Harry's class, 4B, was visiting the British Museum in London for facts about the Romans.

On his journey, he spotted many things: a penny farthing; a WWII gas mask; Roman helmets and different coins from different eras of time."

"Now class, follow me and I will show you something VERY exciting!" exclaimed Harry's teacher, Mr Brownlee, in his loud, Irish accent.

He didn't want to go!

Lola, one of his best friends, spotted him staring into a glass case containing several gold coins. "Harry, let's go. We need to follow Mr Brownlee!" exclaimed Lola, with a worried expression.

He didn't listen.

The brave youngster opened the glass case, leaned over and grasped the glimmering coin.

Suddenly, Lola shouted, "Harry, put th…"

A white mist began to surround him as the golden coin began to evaporate.

After a few seconds, the mysterious mist began to fade as Harry looked around in confusion.

Large, marble statues and luxurious villas were spread as far as the eye could see. People in white robes and toga's strode past him, staring and laughing at him. Impressive men, with red and gold armour marched past him whilst large chariots dragged by black horses raced by.

Harry knew he wasn't in the museum anymore and began to look around.

All of a sudden, a raggedy-clothed child raced past, knocking Harry on the cobbled street floor. After he realised what had just happened, Harry began to chase after the boy. Dodging all obstacles in his way, he began to slow down and panted continuously until he couldn't see the mysterious figure anymore. He began to walk slowly along the street, wondering how he would get back.

All of a sudden, the raggedy boy began running towards him again.

"Oy, you, slow down!" screamed Harry.

Strangely, the boy stopped and replied, "Help me! I'm in trouble with the Emperor Caesar! My name is Octavious and I was his servant. I disobeyed him and now I am in trouble. Help!"

Harry knew just what to do.

He grabbed Octavious by the hand and dragged him behind a nearby pillar. "Wait here, okay?" said Harry, as he began to search the area for the red and gold soldiers.

He walked around, in search for Caesar's soldiers.

All of a sudden, a tall stranger approached him and asked, "Have you seen a boy with a rough head of hair and a set of rags?"

Of course, Harry said no and walked back to the pillar.

"He's gone!" exclaimed Harry.

By Chloe Long

"This is really boring," moaned Lily, who was revising for a history test on World War II. Books didn't seem to be helping and they were so boring too.

Her gran got up from her big armchair, and began to walk to where the door to the attic was.

Confused, Lily followed her gran,

"What are you doing, Gran?" Lily said, with a puzzled look.

"You'll see," Gran replied, and started to bring a large cardboard box down.

"Wow!" Lily began, "is this from when you were little?"

Smiling, her gran nodded her head and began to take out clothes and a gas mask.

"Take a look at the objects, they might help," her gran told her.

The young girl began looking at the clothes, she wanted to know what it would be like to wear them. Thinking that her gran wouldn't mind she put on a black skirt, and a white T-shirt on.

"I don't think that's…" he gran had begun, before she was walking into another room with another box.

Lily was sent into a world of dizziness and thought she was in a dream. But, when she woke up she was still in her gran's house but her gran was not there.

A shiver ran up her spine, when all of a sudden a voice came from the kitchen saying, "Hurry up… we are going now."

Lily ran to the kitchen where a lady and a small child were waiting with a suitcase. They both began to walk outside so she followed.

Lily jumped into a car, which looked a lot like the car that her gran had when she was younger. Jumping into the car, Lily looked back and saw that it looked different.

"Where are we going?" Lily asked.

"What a stupid question, you know where we are going," the lady said.

Lily looked closer at the lady. She looked a lot like her gran's mum. After a long journey, Lily ended up at a large train station.

"Hurry, or the train will have left by the time you get there!" she said.

Lily ran to the station were hundreds, even thousands, of children were standing. Pushing to the front, she grabbed her suitcase, ran into the crowd and waited for a train.

Although she knew the train would be there any minute, above all the noise she could just hear screaming. Looking around, Lily could see that one of the houses was on fire. She ran as fast as she could towards the house, before hearing another scream.

A small girl was inside, about the same age as Lily.

"Please help!" she said, crying. "My legs trapped."

Trying to pull out a large piece of wood, the girl started crying and coughing even more. Eventually, after about a minute, the wood moved and the girl rolled out.

Once outside, the girl began talking, "My name's Suzie. I only went back for my doll. I couldn't leave her, I have had her since I was a baby."

"I'm Lily, I understand, don't worry you're safe now."

Because she got hot, Lilly took off her jumper.

She was then sent back into a world of dizziness.

Once she woke up, she was back in her gran's house. Puzzled, Lily thought that it was maybe, just a dream.

When her gran walked back into the room, she gave her a big hug. "Gran, it's you," she said, smiling.

"Well, who did you think I was?!" she said, laughing. Slowly, she walked over to her armchair and sat down.

"I had a friend called Suzie when I was younger, she was an evacuee, just like me, her house caught fire," her gran said.

"But she was fine, she got saved!" Lily said.

Gran gave a puzzled stare. "How do you know?" the gran asked.

"Oh, you must have said about her before, told me the whole story," Lily said, smiling.

By Izzy Spencer

"Come on, Louis," said Granddad, his deep crusty voice grumbled though the empty air of the museum.

Louis ran along in his untied converse shoes, which seemed like they were about to trip him over. As he was doing so, Louis spotted a sign nearby the exhibit that Granddad was interested in. It read 'Costume Area.'

"Ooh, I want to go in there!" said Louis.

Granddad and Louis entered the room, it was filled with scattered clothing of all different colours, sizes and patterns.

Excitedly, Louis ran towards what seemed to be an old dusty pair of goggles. He grasped it firmly and picked it up. To his surprise, it was not just a pair of goggles, it was a froggy-green gas mask.

"Ha, ha," said Granddad.

"They look just like the real ones!"

Louis asked if he could try it on – Granddad, of course, said yes...

"Hey that looks great, you look just..." said Granddad.

But, Louis could only just hear him over a deafening whirl that echoed around the atmosphere. Choking smoke coated his throat as a large building collapsed in front of him. The rubble was alight with a raging fire that drifted towards the gloomy, grey sky.

Louis turned to his right, where he saw crowds of people, all sprinting in one direction. He turned to his left and saw nothing but a mist of grainy ash. Suddenly, Louis realised that the crowd of running people where running towards him. They were very close now and they would trample him. He quickly took action and dashed out of the way. The blur of uncontrollable body parts washed by him and galloped away from Louis.

All of a sudden, something caught his eye. On the ground beneath him lay a trampled young boy in need of help. His skin was covered with awful bruises, not to mention the long jagged cut through his leg. It was covered with ash and dirt, but Louis could just about see that underneath it was red raw.

"AAaah!" screamed the boy, "help, help!"

Louis immediately jumped down and confronted the little youngster, he only looked about 7 years old but he was oddly familiar! By this time, the boy was crying his eyes out in pain, so Louis carefully helped him over to a little hidey-hole where he could rest.

"Are you okay?" asked Louis (wondering what was going on).

"It really hurts, but that's not important! We must get to the shelter before it's too late!"

Louis was confused, weren't they sheltered already…?

"QUICK!" shouted the boy, "LET'S GO!"

Louis ran as quickly as he could, whilst carrying the weak boy in his arms. Finally, they reached an underground shelter, Louis suddenly realised it was an air raid shelter! The two boys slumped on the floor in exhaustion, and panted for the very little oxygen.

"Who are you?" asked Louis.

"Well, my name is George Wilson Smith, but please call me George."

"That's my Granddad's name!!!" Louis said in a puzzled way. "By the way, I'm Louis."

Just at the moment, someone shouted out the words, "GAS MASKS."

As he heard this, Louis watched everyone else in the room strap on their masks. Louis followed them and put his one on…

"…like me!" said Granddad.

Louis took it off to find himself back in the costume room with Granddad.

"Granddad! It was amazing! There was these people and the building crashing down and the boy – George Wils…!" Louis stopped.

"Calm down, little laddy, I think that's enough in the costume area."

Louis knew who the boy was – it was Granddad!"

He best just keep it a secret though!

By Ella Harmony Topping

"As you know, we will be starting our new history project today," Mrs Avery bellowed.

The new and (meant-to-be) exciting project was World War Two, the period of time Lucy hated most.

"I am going to find a box of props from the cupboard. I'm only popping outside to the resources area so I want you all to remain quiet."

Lucy was bored to death of rules, it was all do this and don't do that. Why can't teachers let you get on with the things you want to do?

Once Mrs Avery had come back into the room, carefully placed all the objects onto the table and put the box to one side, she announced that they could try on the objects if they could work out their proper name.

Unfortunately, Lucy was a know it all at World War Two because she had already done it five years in a row, which was why it was so boring.

She hesitated, and then put her hand up for the first object that had been carefully laid out on the old wooden table.

The teacher scanned the room for any other possible victims she could ask a question. When she realised that no-one else was willing to put their hand up she asked Lucy and she answered correctly.

She stood up and walked to the front waiting to have the gas mask placed over her head.

No sooner was she wearing the mask, than she felt dizzy and a whirling sensation.

Without warning, she found herself in a smoky place. Craters filled with house bricks lined the street. All she could see was demolished houses and scattered rubble scattered along what looked like a road.

Suddenly, she heard a scream. It was coming from a half scattered house. Immediately, her instincts told her to go and help the soul. But, her mind said differently. In the end, she thought it was the right thing to do. As she lifted up some of the bricks, she realised she was stuck in an aid raid shelter and not the actual house, which made the job ten times harder.

She had to work quickly, but carefully, if she was to get her out as she had only a short space of time until a bomb dropped. Slowly, Lucy pulled open the door and grabbed a hand. Suddenly, all the bricks came tumbling down and blocked the doorway…

As soon as the bricks had closed the door, and air raid siren sounded. Now, they knew they were in big trouble. They yelled and called for help. As soon as they knew this wasn't going to get them out, she told the girl, who she found out to be called Sally, to shout and bang in the hope someone would hear them so they could get out.

About ten minutes later, they heard someone outside moving the bricks. Could they be saved?

Soon after, the girls were alert that someone was going to help them. They tried pushing the door open to help some more of the bricks to move away.

Moments later, they were free.

They thanked Officer Fredrickson, the person that had saved them.

He wasn't happy, but wasn't angry at them.

He shouted to them, "Run to the schools air raid shelter, it will be safe there."

As Lucy had no idea where they were going, she decided to let Sally lead the way.

When they reached the air raid shelter, they were instructed to place their gas masks on to their heads.

Lucy panicked when she didn't have one, but then Sally said, "What's that hanging out of your back pocket then?"

And sure enough there was the exact same gas mask Mrs Avery had given to her in class.

Suddenly, she felt a whirling sensation and a dizzy one, exactly the same as she had before she arrived.

"Now, can anyone tell me what this is a picture of?" said Mrs Avery, pointing at the second object on the table.

Lucy looked at it. It was a picture of Mr Fredrickson standing at the air raid shelter they had been trapped in and him trying to dig all the bricks away.

Lucy didn't say anything and instead just gave the class her puzzled face, so no-one would discover that she was inside the air raid shelter a few moments ago.

Without warning, she found herself in a smoky place. Craters filled with house bricks lined the street. All she could see was demolished houses and scattered rubble scattered along what looked like a road.

Suddenly, she heard a scream. It was coming from a half scattered house. Immediately, her instincts told her to go and help the soul. But, her mind said differently. In the end, she thought it was the right thing to do. As she lifted up some of the bricks, she realised she was stuck in an aid raid shelter and not the actual house, which made the job ten times harder.

She had to work quickly, but carefully, if she was to get her out as she had only a short space of time until a bomb dropped. Slowly, Lucy pulled open the door and grabbed a hand. Suddenly, all the bricks came tumbling down and blocked the doorway…

As soon as the bricks had closed the door, and air raid siren sounded. Now, they knew they were in big trouble. They yelled and called for help. As soon as they knew this wasn't going to get them out, she told the girl, who she found out to be called Sally, to shout and bang in the hope someone would hear them so they could get out.

About ten minutes later, they heard someone outside moving the bricks. Could they be saved?

Soon after, the girls were alert that someone was going to help them. They tried pushing the door open to help some more of the bricks to move away.

Moments later, they were free.

They thanked Officer Fredrickson, the person that had saved them.

He wasn't happy, but wasn't angry at them.

He shouted to them, "Run to the schools air raid shelter, it will be safe there."

As Lucy had no idea where they were going, she decided to let Sally lead the way.

When they reached the air raid shelter, they were instructed to place their gas masks on to their heads.

Lucy panicked when she didn't have one, but then Sally said, "What's that hanging out of your back pocket then?"

And sure enough there was the exact same gas mask Mrs Avery had given to her in class.

Suddenly, she felt a whirling sensation and a dizzy one, exactly the same as she had before she arrived.

"Now, can anyone tell me what this is a picture of?" said Mrs Avery, pointing at the second object on the table.

Lucy looked at it. It was a picture of Mr Fredrickson standing at the air raid shelter they had been trapped in and him trying to dig all the bricks away.

Lucy didn't say anything and instead just gave the class her puzzled face, so no-one would discover that she was inside the air raid shelter a few moments ago.

By Michael Wester

"So, how was it like when you were born, Grandpa?'

"Oh, very comfortable and relaxing."

Nick was trying to learn about what it was like for his grandparents. He had talked to Granny about World War II, now he was talking to his Grandpa about the Edwardian times.

"Oh, Nick, I was looking around in the attic and I found some things you might just like. I'll just go get it,' and he trundled out the room.

A minute later, he came back with a box. It had a model boat, a wooden plank... and a gramophone.

"Wow, I've never seen this before," Nick said enthusiastically.

"Yes, I thought you might..." his voice was replaced by a loud beeping noise.

Nick looked around. There were several boats sailing out.

"Come on, come on," a voice said behind him.

He turned to see a line of people behind him.

"Gaa, gaa," a little baby cried.

With a jolt, Nick recognised his grandpa from his baby photos. Nick looked more intently and recognised the cars from his card set.

He walked forward and some men grabbed him. "Come on, get on your ship."

"But, I don't hav..."

"Number 37," the man bellowed at him.

Nick looked at the numbers and quickly found the number 37. He climbed on and set the gramophone down.

A boy walked up to him and said, "Ahh, you'll be the new boy."

Nick nodded and the other boy smiled and said, "We'll be racing – you a good steerer?"

Nick nodded and a bang went off.

"Cripes, we'd better get ready."

Nick went to the steering wheel.

A man got up on a platform and held a gun up.

BANG!!! The gun went off.

"Start steering!" the boy yelled.

Nick tugged on the wheel and the ship started off. Luck was against them as they tore through the storm.

CRACK!!! Lightning smashed the rigging… and it started to burn.

"Take the wheel!" Nick yelled.

"What are you going to do?' the boy yelled back.

"Douse the sails," Nick replied.

Nick slid down the stairs and sent bucketful after bucketful at the sails.

Finally, the sails were dry and picking up wind. They tore into the docks and got out.

"Thanks, my name's John McIllon," John said as they got out.

Nick bent to pick up the gramophone.

The beeping vanished.

"...like it," Grandpa said.

"Grandpa!!!" Nick yelled.

"Who do you think it was, the man on the moon? Captain Nemo?" Grandpa chuckled. "You're holding the gramophone. It reminded me of a boy I knew – John McIllon was his name. He got into some bother as a boy. His ship was set on..."

"Fire by some lightning," Nick interrupted.

"Yes, that's correct, but how did you know?" Grandpa looked befuddled.

"You told me all about it when you were talking about ship disasters."

Grandpa looked even more confused.

"Listen, Grandpa, I think I've got another great project."

About VANESSA WESTER

Vanessa Wester decided to compile GURNARD'S BOOK OF DELIGHTS after she ran a literary competition to celebrate World Book Day 2013 at Gurnard Primary School. On World Book Day, Vanessa presented the school with two signed copies of *The Bother in Burmeon* by S.P. Moss. She challenged the school children to write a story involving time travel, and some did.

The imagination these children showed has been fantastic, and the effort taken by the younger ones to illustrate their stories has been impressive. All children received a certificate, and some The Bother in Burmeon goodies kindly donated by S.P. Moss, who subsequently agreed to judge the Years 4 and 5 entries for an overall winner. Vanessa judged the Reception to Year 3 entries. These overall winners received a £5 Amazon Voucher donated by Vanessa.

DETECTIVE GLEN was written specifically for this collection. Vanessa would like to thank Sir Arthur Conan Doyle for creating the characters of Sherlock Holmes and Watson, which have gone on to inspire many other crime writers to explore a range of ideas.

Vanessa has worked in business, had a career as a Secondary School Mathematics Teacher, which she loved, and finally devoted her time to the upbringing of her children, whilst giving up a lot of her time for voluntary organisations. She still teaches maths as a private tutor and, being a qualified A.S.A. Swimming Teacher, volunteers on weekends at her local swimming club.

Writing is her passion. The day she decided to start writing again was the day she found an outlet for her imagination. It is the best way she can think of to express herself and escape from everyday life.

Vanessa is an author of mainly adult and young adult fiction. Her debut novel, HYBRID (The Evolution Trilogy) was published in May 2012 via Amazon. Since then she has published COMPLICATIONS, the second book in the Trilogy, and has also released another short story called FIRST DATE, which is based on her true story. In addition, she publishes short story collections to aid charity.

Her latest collection of children's short stories, written by a range of authors in aid of the N.S.P.C.C., is called READING IS MAGIC.

She now lives on the Isle of Wight, UK.

DETECTIVE GLENDA

By Vanessa Wester

The most hardened criminal would have been intimidated by Glenda as she stomped around the house, cheeks aflame, huffing and puffing. Her face, as bright and shiny as a cherry, complemented her hair perfectly. Glenda was on the warpath. If no-one was prepared to hear what she had to say, she would make herself heard – just in a different way. It took her all of twenty minutes to realise it would not make the slightest bit of difference. She would have to suffer in silence. That was unless she could come up with a plan.

Lips pursed, eyes narrowed, she eased up to the window. With her back to the wall, she eased her head over her shoulder and peeked out. She had a perfect view of the street. Her cover was exceptional, if she could say so herself. Even though no-one outside could hear her she took slow considered breaths and watched, her mind noting every detail.

There were big boxes, small boxes, lots of furniture, a set of black (perhaps leather) sofas, and a gigantic flat screen television (possibly 3D). They had a lot of cool stuff.

She erased the thought and concentrated on the mission at hand.

The new neighbours were moving in… the suspicious new neighbours. They had arrived just as she had finished her last year of Primary School. She had the whole summer to enjoy and now she had to watch her back every time she went out.

There was also a new boy of about her age. His ripped jeans, hooded top and sunglasses made him look *dodgy*. She had seen him loitering on the driveway, kicking stones. He had seen her as she made her way in from the car to the front door and stared at her, the cheek of it. She had every right to walk to her house. He had no right to watch her. His eyes burned a set of holes in the back of her head, but she did not turn around. She did not dare look until now. From the brief glimpse she got, she *knew* he was the wrong sort, the shifty kind. She would not be making friends with him anytime soon.

Of course, no-one else in the family shared her view that a new set of neighbours signalled the end of the world. The point was *she* did not want *new* neighbours. She wanted her friend, Louise, back. *Louise* was her friend. She did not think she would be able to play with *that* boy, he would *never* replace Louise.

'For crying out loud, what are you doing now Glen?'

Glen jumped, and kicked the huge, glass vase. She dived down and managed to save it before it smashed. She stood up straight, resumed her position and pressed her whole body against the wall, head back. Through gritted teeth, she whispered, 'Dad, they can hear us! Don't give my cover away!'

'Glen, for goodness sakes, you should be glad to have some new neighbours. Apparently, they have a couple of kids, a girl and a boy. The girl's your age. Aren't you glad to have someone new to play with?' he grinned and continued, 'you never know – one of them might be into your spy stuff.'

Glenda gasped in horror as the boy glanced in her direction; he must have seen the curtain move. She threw her hands up in the air. 'Dad, you've just blown my cover. That's just great. And by the way, it's not *just* spy stuff. Someday, I'm going to be the greatest detective the world has ever seen. You'll see.' She folded her arms across her chest and stormed off. She hated being eleven. It was the halfway house to nowhere. She was too young to be an adult, and yet, too old to be a child.

Once in the sanctuary of her room, she pressed play on her iPod docking station and put the volume on high. Then she grabbed her notepad and wrote everything down. It was important to keep a record for future use.

It was also important to update.

Walkie talkie in hand, she pressed the button to talk, 'Red, are you in, I repeat, red are you in?'

A muffled sound followed, 'Oh. Okay.' A giggle. 'Red in, what's your progress blue?'

'The package has landed – I repeat the package has landed.'

A near screech followed, 'COOL! Err, I mean. That's good blue. By the way, my mum wanted to know if you wanted to come over for a sleepover tonight.'

Hannah. You could always rely on her to break ranks.

With a huge sigh, Glenda pressed the button again, determined to keep up her side of the act, 'Affirmative red, sounds like a plan. What time for commencement?'

'You're classic Glen, I mean blue. Say seven o'clock.'

'Over and out.'

Glenda threw herself back on the bed and shut her eyes. Being a detective was hard work. She needed a professional sidekick. Like Watson to Sherlock Holmes,

Gnasher to Dennis, Ron to Harry. Hannah was the best she could get at the moment. She would have to do. Hannah was her best friend after all.

The thing was a serious detective needed a serious partner. She would have to talk to Hannah again, to explain the *situation*. Either way, a sleepover was the perfect chance to have a *tête-à-tête*.

Glenda made her way to the banister and hollered downstairs, 'Mum, Dad, can I have a sleepover at Hannah's tonight?' Her voice sounded like a boom box.

A muffled sound replied.

Impatient, she asked again, 'MUUUUM, DAAAAD, SO CAN I?'

Her mum came out into the hallway, tea towel in her hand, 'Glenda dear, do you have to scream like that?'

Glenda shrugged her shoulders. It was not her fault they were deaf.

'Come down if you want something,' her mum said, as she turned and walked away.

Reluctant, she started to stomp down the stairs. Then she had a change of heart. If she was carefree, happy, they would let her go for sure.

'Hey, Mum,' she said, her voice as light and chirpy as she could muster.

Her mum turned, one eye cocked to the side, 'What do you want then?' She was on to her.

At least her mum was smiling, it was promising.

'The thing is…err… Hannah was wondering if I could go to hers for a sleepover.' Glenda's eyes were wide as she tried to pull off her best puppy dog face. 'So, can I?'

Her dad grimaced, 'Tonight?'

'Yeeees.'

Her mum shrugged her shoulders, 'It's the school holidays after all, why not. Just promise me one thing, no more spying on the neighbours.'

'Promise, Mum.' Behind her back Glenda's fingers were crossed. Everyone knew it negated the promise. To show her appreciation she rushed towards her mum, enveloped her in a gigantic hug and then whizzed off. She had a lot to do.

*

Glenda sat in the corner of Hannah's room deep in thought. The view from Hannah's house was even better than from her house. She had every intention of continuing the surveillance job she had started.

'Can I plait your hair?' Hannah asked, brush in hand. Since Hannah had been brushing her own hair for the last twenty minutes, it did not surprise Glenda that she needed to move on another victim.

Glenda looked up and scrunched her nose, 'There's nothing wrong with my hair.'

In truth, there was – it was sticking up in all the wrong places.

'Come on, I'll make it nice. I don't get to practice on anything other than my doll's head.'

'The WHAT?' Glenda scowled, a deep frown set on her face.

'My *head*, silly.' Hannah picked up a life size model of a head. The hair was braided with coloured ribbons and decorated with an assortment of beads.

Glenda could not believe how girlie Hannah was. It amazed her they were best friends. 'Ugh! Who got you that?'

'My Aunt, of course, she knows I love to play with hair.'

'Fine, you can do mine. BUT, after that we get down to business. Promise?' Glenda narrowed her eyes, shoulders hunched.

Hannah gave a girlie giggle. 'I promise. You're funny Glen, or should I still call you Red?'

'Whatever,' Glenda sighed, turned round and released her long, curly red hair from the tight bands normally keeping it together.

Hannah came up behind her, 'This is a challenge, even for me. You're not going to scream like a baby when I find tangles, are you?'

'NO.' Glenda held her head up high.

'Good.'

Five minutes later, Glenda was in agony. After ten, she had lost the will to live.

'Are you done, yet?'

'I knew you'd end up complaining,' Hannah sighed. 'Anyway, I'm done. Have a look.' Hannah handed over a pink hand mirror.

'AHHH...'

'It's not that bad,' Hannah pouted, arms folded.

'I look like a poodle, what do you mean? It's not that

bad. It's hideous. I knew I shouldn't have let you loose on my hair.'

The sound of Hannah's mum's voice interrupted the moment, 'Hannah, Glenda, can you come downstairs please. We have visitors.'

'What am I going to do?' Glenda screeched, hands over her head. It would take ages to untie all the braids and get rid of the bows.

'Towel!' Hannah said, as she tossed a large, purple one over. 'Put it on your head, like a turban, we'll pretend you washed your hair.'

'Argh, it'll have to do.' Glenda wrapped the towel round her head and prayed whoever it was would go away soon.

Hannah got down first. Glenda tentatively followed, fingers crossed behind her back. There were an awful lot of voices coming from the lounge.

'Hannah, there you are. Where's Glenda? Is she coming?'

Thwarted! Glenda secretly hoped they'd forgotten all about her.

She walked very slowly and cruised through the door. The sight of an entire group of strangers, as well as Hannah's parents and brother, left her speechless. A pair of eyes hovered somewhere amongst the melee, probing her. Instinctively, she turned to face them – deep blue, curly blonde hair, cool hooded top, jeans and a slight smirk. It was the boy from next door. If anyone had caught her watching it was *him*. And by the look he gave her, she knew he *knew*. He had caught her red handed, and now, with that sly look, he was making her pay.

'Glenda, right?' Another set of blue eyes, this time surrounded by a scattering of freckles. The girl's hair was also blonde, but it hung loose, past her shoulders. 'I'm Penny.'

She had to be his sister.

As Hannah's parents introduced everyone Glenda stood in silence. The boy's name was Matthew. Typical, he had a biblical name even though he did not look saintly.

Hannah gave her an odd look. She ignored her. When Hannah stamped on her foot Glenda blurted out, 'Nice to meet you.'

Eventually, Hannah's parents asked them to show Penny and Matthew the playroom. Glenda felt like laughing, they were too old to have a *playroom*. Glenda tried to think of what she could do with her hair, she could not walk around with a towel for hours. Hannah started chatting to Penny, Matthew skulked after them. Glenda kept quiet and trailed behind. The way he walked was interesting. It was like a shuffle and a hop – almost rhythmical.

She took a quick detour into the toilet, quickly undid the towel and hastily took off all the ribbons. Then she tied up her hair in a bun, it would have to do. She made her way over to the playroom.

The playroom was massive. It was stacked with toys, board games, a table and chairs, a comfy sofa, and a flat screen television with loads of gadgets attached. Hannah went straight for her collection of Polly Pockets, Penny followed. Matthew seemed to nod in approval and made for the TV, immediately drawn to the PS3.

Glenda was torn.

She did not want to play with the Polly Pockets – she wanted to play on the PS3. She just did not want to play with *him*. Unfortunately, it didn't look like she had much choice.

'What game are you going to play?' she asked. She sounded far too pathetic. She needed to boost her voice next time. She wanted him to know she was confident.

Matthew barely looked up, 'Don't know.'

'What about this one?' Glenda held up one of her favourites, *Road Rage*.

He scrunched up his face, she noticed he had a scattering of cute freckles on his nose, and said, 'you like that one?'

'Yeah, why wouldn't I?' She shook her head. 'What 'cause I'm a *girl*?'

'You said it, not me.' He actually smiled.

It made a butterfly flutter in her stomach. No boy had ever made that happen before. 'So, shall we play?'

'Sure.'

An hour later, they were in fits of laughter on the sofa, after a million car destructions and a series of competitive games. Glenda had reassessed, he was not bad after all even if he was *just* a boy.

'So, what are you doing for the summer?' Glenda asked. She could not help asking another question, 'Where are you from anyway?' Matthew had a strange accent.

He smiled again and put the console down. 'That's two questions.'

Glenda grinned.

'Okay, we are staying here for the summer. As far as I know we haven't got a lot planned. We used to live in Rotterdam.'

Her jaw dropped, he lived in a foreign country – at least she was sure it was not in England. 'Rotterdam, I've heard of that… where is it again?'

'In The Netherlands or Holland as it's more commonly known.'

Her jaw dropped wider, 'WOW. Do you speak a different language then?'

'Yes, I also speak Dutch, funnily enough,' he chuckled.

Glenda's eyes widened. 'Say something then. Please?'

'Hoe gaat het met je.'

Glenda could not help giggling. 'What does *that* mean?'

Penny seemed to remember them all of a sudden, 'Nice to meet you.'

'Oh, right. Same.' Glenda was sure she was blushing.

'So, what do you all do here for fun?' Matthew asked.

Hannah was quick to reply, 'We are detectives.'

'Detectives?' Matthew said, as he laughed and Penny giggled.

'Glenda has a wicked imagination,' Hannah said, as she joined in with their joke.

Glenda started to blush. She was being ganged up on. 'Genius is never acknowledged until proven. You'll see. I will be the best detective there has ever been.' She stomped out of the room and headed upstairs to Hannah's room. She would stew in there for a while. She felt humiliated.

Five minutes later, Hannah knocked on the door and then made her way in. 'I shouldn't really knock to come into my own bedroom, but I think I upset you. Sorry.'

'It's alright.' Glenda sat up on the bed.

'What was that all about? They're nice enough. We weren't making fun of you. It was your face, so serious.'

'I was just trying to show off. Don't worry about it.' Glenda turned away and looked out the window.

Hannah moved towards Glenda and stood in front of her. 'It didn't sound like you were showing off. I don't doubt you, one day you will be the best detective ever.'

Glenda stood her ground. 'I doubt that.'

Hannah pouted. 'None of that. The Glenda I know doesn't doubt her abilities.'

'Look I'm sorry. I think maybe I should go home.'

Hannah smiled. 'Don't be silly. My mum makes the best hot chocolate, marshmallows and cream you'll ever have.'

'Okay, I can't say no to that. The thing is if the new neighbours are actually nice, then who are we going to investigate?'

Hannah tapped her head, and said, 'I'm sure you'll come up with something.'

Glenda stared into the distance. The day had killed some of her spirit, but some lingered. She was sure a hot chocolate might be just what she needed to perk up.

*

The next day Glenda trudged back home with her sleepover bag. She had not slept very long, since Hannah talked incessantly. The topic of conversation had centred a lot on the new neighbours. She thought Penny was really nice, and her brother was dishy. Glenda rolled her eyes at the thought. She was too young to think of boys, in any shape or form. As far as she was concerned they were annoying, arrogant and dirty. She knew it was bad to generalise, but all the boys she knew at school fit the bill, or some of it.

Just as she was about to knock on her front door, she heard a voice behind her. She glanced over her shoulder, a scowl pasted on her face. 'What do you want?'

'Look, I'm sorry,' Matthew began, 'we didn't mean to upset you yesterday. I just wanted to say that. So, are we cool?' He shuffled from one foot to the other.

He had wet hair, was wearing a smart shirt and beige trousers, and stared at her with big eyes.

'Are you seriously apologising?' Her mouth gaped open.

He smiled, two cute dimples on display, and said, 'of course.'

Glenda squirmed slightly and felt the blood rush to her cheeks. He was a boy, he was admitting he was wrong, he looked clean, and he was not being annoying. He was breaking all of her ideals. She didn't like it.

'Apology accepted,' she said, as she held back a yawn. Her eyelids were really heavy now. She blinked a few times.

'Sorry if I bore you,' he raised his eyebrows.

'No,' she snapped, 'sorry, I just didn't get much sleep. You know what it's like... sleepover.'

'Yeah, I get it,' he smiled again, and kicked a stone lightly away. 'Anyway, I wanted to tell you that my parents really love detective stuff. They have loads of old books, movies and ornaments. They have been collecting for years. Well, I, err, told my parents you liked detective stuff and they said we could unload the box if we were careful and put it all away for them.'

Glenda was lost for words for a moment. All she managed was a feeble, 'oh.'

'So, anyway, maybe another day when you're not so tired,' he said, and then turned to walk away.

Glenda found her voice, 'That would be great. I can come round later, after I've had a rest.'

Matthew glanced back, 'Later then.'

Glenda waited until he was out of sight and then knocked on the front door. The last thing she wanted was to admit to her parents that the neighbour's son was actually alright. Although, she did not know how she was going to explain where she was going later on. She would have to say Penny invited her. It was only a small fib.

*

Glenda could not believe she was about to go to a boy's house. She could excuse it as research, and if anyone asked that is what she would say. If it had not been the summer holiday's homework would have been an excellent decoy. Within a metre of the door she hesitated. She doubted any of the stuff his parents had would be interesting but she was too curious to give it a miss. Matthew had invited her after all. Then again, what if he was just being polite? She scowled, bit her lip and turned round to go back home.

She had moved a few paces when she heard the door open behind her and Matthew call out, 'changed your mind.'

Glenda could feel the heat on her cheeks. She placed her cool hands on her face, then dropped them and turned around. 'No, I just wasn't sure anyone was home.'

'But you hadn't even knocked,' he smirked, his arms folded over his chest as he leaned against the door frame, one foot over the other.

'I... err..,' she scratched her head. 'Hang on a minute,' Glenda paused, and scowled as she thought. She took a step forward. 'How did you know I was here?'

Matthew's face remained devoid of emotion, 'I happened to look out.'

'Really?'

'Yes, really,' Matthew rolled his eyes. 'So, are you coming in?'

Glenda still did not know if she could truly trust him. The logical part of her brain told her to go back home immediately, the reckless part pushed her towards Matthew.

Once inside, she lingered in the doorway. A lot of boxes remained sealed at the entrance.

'Ignore the mess,' Matthew said, as he waved her forward.

'Well, you only just moved in,' Glenda said.

'Mum said the box with the detective stuff was in the attic. Do you want a drink or something before we go up there?'

Glenda tried to suppress her surprise at his consideration. Through a croaky voice, she replied, 'no, thank you.'

'Your voice sounded funny there, maybe a glass of water after all,' he grinned.

'Humph, there is nothing wrong with my voice. Are you always this *nice*?' she blurted out. She had never been one to keep quiet.

'Of course,' he replied, in a voice laced with silk. 'Go on then, let's get crackin' or it'll get late.'

Glenda bit her tongue and walked after him. Her curiosity overpowered the need to thump him on the back.

His house was much bigger and much older than hers. It had three storeys and the attic room had proper stairs, not ones you pulled out like she had. He flicked the light switch and they slowly made it up the winding staircase. It was quite steep and narrow but it did the job.

The attic was full of boxes already; although some in the corner were so dusty she reckoned they belonged to a previous owner.

'This is it,' Matthew said, as he peeled off the thick, sticky tape sealing the box.

Glenda stood next to him and peeked in. The eerie silence of the room made her uncomfortable.

Matthew started taking all sorts of things out of the box. Dress up costumes, books, pens, all sorts themed in a detective range.

Glenda giggled. 'This is not *serious* stuff.'

'And your stuff is?' he gave a half smile, and glanced at her.

'Maybe,' she mused, her eye drawn to the dusty corner of the room. 'Let's see what else is lurking in your attic.'

'We don't know what that stuff is. Apparently, it's been here for years. The previous owners said we were welcome to it. My parents did not look too happy to keep it, but it was easier to say okay,' he explained. 'Personally, I think that's what they told me. They love to browse through old stuff.'

'I think I like your parents,' Glenda smiled.

'Hmmm, they're alright.'

Glenda started pushing the dusty boxes aside, keen to see what was behind them. Her hands felt rough from the dust, but she carried on. She was on the hunt for clues.

'You're not going to find anything,' Matthew sighed, now tight behind her.

Glenda ignored him and focused on a loose floorboard under the boxes she had moved. She started to wiggle it about, and then fell back as it came out.

'Now what have you done?'

Glenda put the floorboard down. 'A good detective leaves no stone unturned, or floorboard in this case.'

'Obviously,' he said, his tone sarcastic. 'What is it?'

Glenda started to pull out a small, biscuit tin. 'No idea.'

She placed it on the floor between them and tried to open the lid, but it was jammed shut.

'Here use this,' Matthew said, as he handed her a metal coat hanger.

Glenda stared at the coat hanger, and narrowed her eyes.

'I'll do it then, 'Matthew said. He took the box, sat down, wedged it between his knees and used the metal coat hanger as a lever. Slowly, the lid started to move until after a few minutes of careful work it flicked off and landed on the floor with a clang.

'What's inside? Let me see,' Glenda said, as she pushed forward.

Matthew held the box away from her, '*I* opened it.'

Glenda gave a massive sigh, as her shoulder slumped.

Matthew turned round. 'You're a huffy kind of girl, aren't you?'

Glenda made to get up and leave.

'Oh, sit down already. I'm only teasing. Look,' he held out the box.

Glenda pursed her lips, her eyes still partially narrowed. She breathed out, and shuffled forward to take a look. She *had* to see what was inside. Pride told her to leave, curiosity made her stay.

When she saw what it was her jaw dropped. 'It can't be.'

'What is it?' Matthew shimmied closer.

Her fingers reached out to touch it. As they curled around the book, she slowly lifted it out of the box. 'I can't believe it.'

'What?'

She carefully placed the book on the floor. Her hand trembled, and her throat went dry.

Matthew read over her shoulder, 'Beeton's Christmas Annual? What is it?'

She stared at the Annual, her eyes wide. She did not want to answer Matthew. She wanted to look at the book. But she knew if she did not answer he would only harass her further. 'It's an original copy of an annual published in 1887. It includes *A Study in Scarlet* written by Sir Arthur Conan Doyle.'

'By *who*?'

Glenda was losing her patience now. She took a deep breath and tried to stay calm, and think happy thoughts. 'Have you heard of Sherlock Holmes?'

'Who?'

'Oh, for goodness sakes…'

Matthew laughed, 'Yes, I've heard of *Sherlock Holmes*.'

'Well, this is the first story ever published that mentions Sherlock Holmes and Watson. It's priceless. There are only meant to be 11 copies of this annual in the world. This could be the twelfth copy.' Her jaw dropped again.

'Well, in that case it's valuable and it belongs to me since it is in *my* house.'

Glenda bit her inner cheek. 'Well, actually it belongs to your parents. But, seriously who cares how much it's worth. This is amazing.' She reached out to touch it, scared stiff. She would never live with herself if she damaged it.

'Hands off,' Matthew said. 'Let's put it back in the box. We don't want to damage it.'

'Now, who's being prissy?' Glenda sneered.

As Matthew reached out to get the book, she snapped again, 'I'll do it.' She carefully placed the book back in the tin box and loosely put on the lid.

'Look, I'm sorry if I'm being weird,' Matthew said, 'it's just, if it is worth a lot of money, well, you know...'

Glenda knew only too well about money, or lack of it more like. 'It's just that... this should not be sold.'

'You don't know my parents will sell it. They might keep it. They love detective stuff too.'

'I guess.'

Matthew stood up and held out his hands for the box. Glenda passed it to him and stood next to him. He walked towards the stairs and Glenda followed. She felt miserable, just like when her dog had died.

As she started to go after him, she lost her footing on the narrow step and could not help herself falling forward onto Matthew.

'Watch it,' he shouted, but it was too late.

They both rolled down the steep staircase and collapsed in a heap at the bottom. The last thing Glenda remembered was something hard hitting her head as she fell.

*

Glenda's eyes fluttered open and she rubbed her head. A small lump throbbed when she pressed her fingers against it. She heard a low groan next to her.

'Matthew?' She turned to face the sound.

Matthew was pushing his body up with his hand, as he shook his head lightly from side to side. '*That* really hurt.'

'Sorry,' she mumbled.

'It's okay,' Matthew said, before a series of words tumbled out if his mouth, 'whatisthisplace? whatisgoingon?'

'Slow down, slow down,' Glenda said as she looked up and found herself facing a grand corridor. The carpet was a vibrant red. The walls were wallpapered, not painted, in a floral pattern. The lights on the walls were an intricate design, made out of a pretty, moulded type of metal, which she assumed to be brass. Glenda was sure she had seen a picture of them at school when they studied Victorian times. They looked like oil lamps.

It certainly *did not* look like the corridor she had passed on the way up to the attic.

'Glenda…'

'I know, I know,' she sighed. 'Just give me a minute to think.'

Matthew stood up and touched the wall, then studied the lamp. 'This is pretty cool.'

Glenda stood up and frowned. 'Where's the tin box?'

'It vanished,' Matthew said, as he started to walk towards the staircase.

'Where are you going?' Glenda hissed.

'Exploring... are you coming? Or are you chicken?' he sneered.

Glenda folded her arms, 'Me? Chicken?' She rolled her eyes, dropped her arms to her sides and strode towards him, head held high.

'Guess not,' Matthew chuckled.

When she got to the banister she hesitated and leaned over to look downstairs. It was still daylight, and the only sound was that of a loud ticking clock.

'Well, go on then,' Matthew said. He swept his arm in front of him. 'Ladies first.'

Glenda was annoyed at his use of chivalry, but she let it slide this once and started down the stairs. The sound of a creaky floorboard made her pause. After a second or two she carried on. It was difficult to go down the wooden stairs quietly. She had never seen stairs without carpet before. A large, oil painting hung on the wall as they made their way down. It was a depiction of a battle scene, with a lot of blood and gore on display. Not her taste.

At the bottom of the staircase, she saw a slightly open door up ahead. Glenda made her way towards it. She glanced at Matthew and edged her head slightly to the side to indicate that she was planning to go in. Matthew frowned and scrunched his eyes together. She could not help a cheeky grin escape. Now Matthew was a chicken. She put her hand out and moved the door inwards. What Glenda saw left her gob-smacked.

She had never seen such an array of chemical equipment in her life. She had no idea what it all was but there were a lot of different sized glass orbs, coloured liquids and small utensils that she had never seen before. It had the look of a laboratory, just not like any she had seen before, even on television.

She made her way up to a table and picked up a stained cloth. It was smudged with dark, brownish stains.

'Don't pick anything up,' Matthew sighed.

'You are such a *chicken*,' Glenda smirked.

'Ha, ha, very funny.' Matthew walked up to the counter and picked up a large magnifying glass. He started to stare into it as he pulled it towards and away from him. Then he put it up close to small objects like some glass beads on the worktop. 'This is amazing. You can see loads more colours up close.'

'Fancy yourself as a bit of a scientist now, huh,' Glenda jibed.

'Come and see.'

Glenda made her way over, took the magnifying glass in her hand and looked up close at the beads. Matthew was right. She had never seen a coloured bead in so much detail. She put it down and walked around the room. She saw a tobacco pipe laid on a small table by a beautifully carved, wooden chair with plump red cushions. There were heaps of papers in bundles all around the room and a bookcase stacked with books. She read through the titles. Forensic science, crime studies, body embalming, weapons of destruction, the study of the mind, such a wide array of grotesque information.

A shiver ran down her spine. She had no idea who would read this. It was all interesting to her, of course, but it was not what she considered to be *average* reading.

She picked out a journal called *Nature* and leafed through the pages. An article written by Henry Faulds had extensive notes all along the margin. It talked of the use of finger prints to solve a crime. Her eyes widened as she flicked back to the front page. The journal had been published in 1880 and it was still in a very good condition. It did not look old *at all*.

A newspaper caught the corner of her eye. 'Matthew, pick up the newspaper. What is the date on it? Quick.'

Matthew picked up the newspaper and scanned for the date. As his eyes fixed on it his mouth gaped open.

'What is the date?' Glenda shouted.

'Shush,' Matthew hissed, 'its 1887 according to this paper.'

Glenda sat on the chair, and lowered her head into her hands, her elbows leaning against her legs. 'Oh no, tell me this is a dream. Please.'

'It's a dream,' Matthew said. 'Can we go home now?'

Glenda raised her head. 'If only.'

The sound of keys jangling made them both jump.

Glenda leapt off the chair, raced towards the door of the room and watched in horror as the main door started to open. 'Too late,' she whispered.

Matthew waved her over, as he held the large curtains open. They both allowed the thick, luscious velvet brown material to swallow them up and they stayed perfectly still. Glenda scarcely breathed.

A set of footsteps made their way into the room. She heard the sound of someone moving around and then heard a deep sigh. 'Watson, have you been touching my things again?'

Glenda suppressed a cough as she heard another pair of footsteps. They sounded slightly heavier than the first.

'What are you on about now, Holmes, my good friend?'

Glenda could not believe what she was hearing. Matthew released a nervous giggle.

'Aha,' the first voice said, 'we have visitors. Please come out.'

'More visitors?' the second voice sounded amused.

'Visitors with a problem, Watson.'

'All your visitors have problems,' Watson joked. 'Well, come on then, out with you.'

Glenda knew they had no choice. She gave a half smile in Matthew's direction as they both left their cover.

'Ah, a young girl and a boy. The girl is not too keen on him at the moment, I see. That might change in a year or so,' he chuckled. 'I am…'

'*Sherlock Holmes*,' Glenda gasped.

'Indeed,' Sherlock nodded, 'a young sleuth.'

'She likes to think so,' Matthew added.

'Ahhh, yes, a mini Watson, right Watson?'

'Indeed,' Watson laughed.

'My name is Glenda, this is Matthew,' Glenda asserted, she raised her head high.

'Confident too, impressive.' Sherlock took a seat, and picked up his tobacco pipe.

Glenda put her hand on her hip. 'I really wouldn't do that.'

'And why not, might I ask?' Sherlock gave an amused chuckle.

'It can kill you,' Matthew said.

'Indeed.' Sherlock glanced at Watson. 'A lot of things can kill me. Tobacco is not one of them.'

'My grandfather died of lung cancer. It's not a joke,' Glenda continued.

'Lung cancer, you say. Grave indeed. Best put it away then, Watson.'

'I think this girl has you all figured out,' Watson said. He picked up the newspaper and flicked through the pages.

'Anyway, we need a cup of tea. Ring the bell, Watson. I suggest you both hide.' Sherlock raised his eyebrows. 'The servant will not be as understanding about whatever you are both wearing.'

Glenda and Matthew resumed their hiding spot. Glenda heard the sound of the servant come in, take their order and leave. She liked the sound of that. It seemed better than takeaway, and was probably a lot quicker too.

Ten minutes later, the door opened again. After a few minutes they were gone.

'You can come out now,' Sherlock said.

When Glenda saw the selection of biscuits on the tray her mouth watered.

'Go ahead, take some,' Watson said, as he held out an empty plate to Glenda and Matthew.

They both filled their plates.

As Glenda was about to take a bite of her favourite garibaldi biscuit she heard a tutting sound. 'What?' she asked.

'Please take a seat. I have never heard anyone say *what* in that manner before. Do you have no manners where you come from?' Sherlock asked.

'Err...' Glenda hesitated.

'Take a seat,' Watson said.

'As you eat, allow me to make some deductions,' Sherlock nodded. 'You are not from here.'

'Even I knew that,' Watson said. His rosy cheeks and eyes brightened.

'Precisely,' Sherlock said, he rubbed his long, narrow chin with his hand. 'Your accent, clothing and mannerisms give you away. However, even though I am an authority on people,' he raised his finger to the air, 'I admit I am stumped.' His shoulders slumped a little.

'And that does not happen often,' Watson said.

'I know,' Glenda mumbled.

'Don't talk with your mouth full, child,' Watson said, a look of horror pasted on his face. 'And what do you mean, you *know*?'

'They know *of* me, Watson. That's obvious. The question is why and how?'

'Obvious,' Watson grumbled, as he hid behind the cover of the newspaper.

'Glenda, Matthew,' he paused and looked from one to the other. 'Please enlighten me. Who are you? This never happens to me, EVER.' He pursed his lips and clasped his long, thin fingers in front of his face.

'I know,' Glenda smiled. She found his apparent frustration entertaining.

'Again! You are an annoying little person, are you not?' Sherlock gave a half smile.

'I try my best,' Glenda smirked.

'Watson, what are we to do with them?' He gave a sinister smile.

Glenda did not like it. She felt goose bumps at the back of her neck.

'Child, tell us where you are from,' Watson pleaded.

Glenda hesitated, and Matthew jumped in. 'This is my house.'

'Your house!' Sherlock chuckled, before he muttered under his breath, 'the audacity of the child.'

'Well, it's my parents', actually,' Matthew said, now even more brazen, 'and they just bought it in 2012. Just in time for the Olympic year. Great time to be in London.'

'The *what* year? Watson, these children must be hallucinating, bring the smelling salts. They need to be revived.'

'Of course,' Matthew continued, with a smile, 'the Olympics started already. It's very exciting, third time in London since 1948. Men and women from all over the world competing for medals, I reckon Britain will get more gold medals this time round. I'll be watching the Dutch at hockey, they're very good.'

Glenda watched Sherlock nod, and stare deep in thought. It was obvious he did not know what to make of it all.

'Did you say *women*?' Watson asked, with a dubious expression.

'Of course,' Matthew said, 'I think if we play our cards right the women will get us some gold medals in the swimming pool, although we've not got off to a great start there.'

'Women swimming in a pool, *with* men?' Watson guffawed.

'No, not *with* men. Women compete against other women, men against other men. It has to be fair,' Matthew explained.

'Fair,' Watson said. He nodded his head and then smiled. 'They'll be saying women can vote next.'

'Actually,' Glenda coughed, 'women can vote, and do pretty much anything men can. Although my mum reckons it's always going to be *harder* for women.'

'And why would that be? Enlighten us,' Sherlock's eyes widened and he moved closer.

'Well,' Glenda said, 'no matter what advancements we have and however hard women fight for equality in the workplace and stuff, we are they only ones that can,' she paused, and then whispered, and mock retched, 'have the *babies*.'

'Equality in the workplace!' Sherlock started to laugh aloud and moved to pick up his tobacco pipe. 'Sorry children, but I have to smoke to that.'

'I need a brandy,' Watson said, his lips drooped at the

edges.

'No, no, Watson. This is all good. Let women vote, work like men, play sport like men, and have the babies. Means men will have less to do, not that I ever intend to get together with a lady friend. I abhor the idea of marriage,' he grimaced.

'Well, I am quite taken with the idea actually. I think it all sounds quite reasonable, although I doubt many women could fight in the battlefield and stay level headed, especially not after what I saw in Afghanistan.'

'That's still a dangerous place. Many soldiers die there today,' Matthew added, seriously.

'And you say you come from the year 2012, did I hear you correctly?' Sherlock mused, as he took a long drag of his cigar.

As he puffed out the smoke, Glenda wrinkled her nose and her throat constricted. It really was the most awful smell.

Matthew replied, 'yes.'

'So, what are we to do with them, Watson?'

'I suggest we send them to bed. It is late, and they're bound to be tired

'Indeed, well they can have your bedroom then. You can sleep on the floor in my room.'

Watson frowned, 'I guess that's the only thing we can do. Go on then, you two, to bed with you. Follow me.'

As they walked out Glenda noticed Sherlock looking out of the window, deep in thought. She thought it was probably the first time anyone had ever caught him off guard.

When they got to the landing, Glenda saw the attic step up ahead. She really didn't want to sleep on Watson's bed, and she really didn't want to share a room with Matthew. She made a run for it and worked her way up to the top. She made her way to the floorboard where they had found the annual and pried it off the floor. It was empty.

'Why are you destroying our property now, child?' Watson shouted. His nostrils flared slightly. 'What's wrong with you?'

'I-It's nothing.' Glenda held back the tears and swallowed.

Watson relented, and beckoned her forward in a soft voice, 'come on then.'

Glenda shuffled behind. When she got to the top of the stair she paused and looked back. A lone tear wandered down her cheek and she brushed it away. She started down the stairs and lost her footing again. She closed her eyes as she fell down and braced herself for the landing.

*

'Glenda, are you awake, Glenda?' her mum's voice called.

Glenda's eyes fluttered open slowly, and she gazed into her mum's face. The walls were all white around her and a disinfectant smell lingered in the air.

'Is she waking up?' her dad this time.

Glenda opened her mouth to speak, and she managed to get some words out, even though her throat was parched. 'Where am I?'

'You are in hospital. You had a nasty fall, but you're going to be okay now,' Mum smiled.

'Where is Matthew?'

'Matthew is at his house. He's perfectly fine. He'll want to know that you are okay though. He was really worried. He thought it was his fault you fell,' Dad explained, 'he said he had upset you.'

Glenda started to cough.

'Here have some water,' her mum said, as she held her head up and placed the glass of water in front of her lips.

Glenda sipped it and relished the cool taste.

'We have some exciting news, Glenda,' her dad said, 'Matthew's parents came to visit you before, but they could not stay. They asked us to tell you that they would like to talk to you about what they should do with the annual.'

Glenda's jaw dropped.

'Matthew told them you found it and so they think you should have a say in what they do with it,' her mum smiled again.

'Fancy that, an *original* copy,' her dad nodded, his eyes wide.

'So, that bit was true,' Glenda closed her eyes. She opened them again and saw her parents' puzzled expressions.

'What do you mean, sweetheart?' her mum asked.

Glenda closed her eyes again and ran her tongue over her teeth. As she dislodged a currant with the buttery taste of the garibaldi biscuit from her back tooth she wondered if it had all been a dream or not.

Either way, she was sure they would never believe her.

She gave a half smile, her eyes focused on the ceiling. 'Nothing, Mum.'

ABOUT S.P. MOSS

Flying and travel are in Susan Moss's blood – she visited four of the world's continents before starting school. She read avidly and wrote determinedly in between plotting to become a spy and building brother-proof camps.

She studied Psychology at Trinity College, Cambridge, taking part in some interesting experiments in parapsychology as well as playing trumpet in a Big Band.

A chance meeting in an Austrian ski hut resulted in more travel – this time to Germany, where she now lives in a small town outside Frankfurt with her husband and son.

She still makes use of her trumpet-playing, spying and camp-building skills in her busy life as an author, mother and freelance marketing consultant.

The Bother in Burmeon was her debut novel. This original adventure story, which manages to be enchanting and exciting at the same time, was the winner of the *Earlyworks Press Novels for Children or Teens Competition*.

Now, as any writer knows, whether you're writing a book or making a film, there are always scenes that don't make it into the final cut. Sometimes they just make the story too long. Or maybe they get in the way of the exciting action that's going on. Susan is honest and admits she *hates* cutting these bits out of her stories. Unlike a film, you normally don't get a chance to see these in the "extras" part.

So for this collection, we are lucky enough to get an

exclusive – two scenes from *The Bother in Burmeon* that ended up on the cutting room floor.

If you've read the story, you'll know it's about a boy who goes back half a century in time to have an adventure with his Grandpop, a young RAF pilot.

These two scenes are about the chaos that ensues when Grandpop lands in the present day – and finds that things are rather different to 1962!

Please enjoy…

THE TO-DO AT TESBURY'S

By S. P. Moss

'Well, there's Tesbury's just on the outskirts of town – on the London Road. You can get anything there,' said Billy in answer to Grandpop's question about where they could buy provisions for their forthcoming mission.

'Roger, old chap. Tesbury's it is, then.'

The little green Austin Healey car swerved and curved its way to the huge supermarket which stood on a sort of desolate island together with a petrol station and a D-I-Y store. Someone had tried to make the landscape a little friendlier with lines of flower beds lining the car park but the effect was still soul-less and dismal. Billy loathed coming shopping to these sorts of places but he imagined with Grandpop things would be a little different.

The Austin Healey screeched to a halt in a parking place just outside Tesbury's entrance.

'Um – Grandpop, you can't park here. It's for disabled,' said Billy.

'Can you get more disabled than being dead, old chap? But we'd better do the decent thing. What about over there?'

'I think that's for mother and baby.' Billy noticed one of the car washers – an older man who nevertheless looked like an overgrown schoolboy – who hung around Tesbury's car park grabbing his cleaning tools rather over-zealously at the sight of the Austin Healey.

'And Grandpop and grandson with an ancient old motor and barking mad dog?' questioned Grandpop. 'Ho hum! That chap with the bucket at twelve o'clock looks a touch alarming – better make ourselves scarce.'

Grandpop swung the little car away from the over-excited gaze of the car washer, spun around the car park ignoring the one-way signs and neatly nipped into a free place.

As Billy, Monty and Grandpop were getting out of the car, Billy noticed a tank-like 4X4 grinding to a halt just before their parking place. Inside, a woman with large sunglasses and lots of jewellery threw up her hands from the steering wheel, gesticulated wildly and appeared to be screaming at someone or something at the top of her voice. She climbed down from the vehicle, which was not easy as she was a large lady, squeezed into a baby pink tracksuit that she appeared to have borrowed from her small daughter and balanced on a precarious pair of high-heeled sandals. Her cautious exit from her tank had obviously taken the wind out of her sails a little as, by the time she teetered over in Billy and Grandpop's direction, she was muttering under her breath rather than screaming.

'Do you make a habit of nicking other people's parking places, then?' she demanded of Grandpop.

'Good afternoon, madam. Squadron Leader Walker, RAF.' Grandpop stretched out his hand, oblivious to the woman's sarcastic tone.

'Yeah, and I'm the Queen of bleedin' Sheba...' the woman muttered and stared at Grandpop's hand, bemused and confused.

'My good lady,' unperturbed, Grandpop took the woman's hand, held it very briefly and then shook it. 'You appear to be in some sort of distress. I only hope that I haven't inadvertently offended you in some way. Is there any way I can be of any assistance to you?' He smiled, charmingly.

'Ooh, well,' the woman gazed down at her hand, then up to Grandpop. The corners of her mouth turned up slightly and she raised her giant sunglasses. Billy detected a slight fluttering of the eyelashes. 'I did have my eye on that parking spot myself – you know how it is – but it really doesn't matter...'

'Goodness gracious! Then you shall have it, my dear lady. I'm most awfully sorry – but your wish is my command!' Grandpop and Billy made their way back to the car. The woman teetered after them.

'Oh, no, no, really, it doesn't matter,' she simpered. 'By the way, hope you don't mind me asking, and I know you said you were Squaddie Leader someone, but aren't you really whatsisname that's just been chosen as the new James Bond? I follow you in the magazines, you know, and I think you'll be just fab!'

Grandpop waved in a friendly manner as he started up the car. Billy could see the woman hurriedly digging into her large white handbag, pulling out a mobile phone and excitedly tapping something into it.

'Very flattering I'm sure but maybe the dear lady needs some sensible spectacles instead of those cinema screens. Now, what about this parking slot?' Grandpop was just about to manoeuvre the Austin Healey into another space when he realised that it was full of the over-excited car washer and his buckets. The man was practically drooling at the mouth at the sight of the classic car and was wildly beckoning Grandpop apparently to park on top of him.

Having found a parking place free of human hazards, Grandpop took Billy in one hand and his pipe in the other, with Monty trotting behind and marched briskly towards Tesbury's.

'Now, old chap,' said Grandpop as they stopped outside the store entrance. 'I must say that I find shopping completely ghastly. I wonder if it wouldn't be asking too much if you'd just pop in and get a few provisions. Now, I did make a list somewhere, unless Monty's chewed it up. Ah, here we are! Corned beef, four tins. Fish paste, two jars. Salmon. Wills' tobacco, best Virginia, two packets. Peek Freans...'

'Um, Grandpop,' Billy butted in, a little reluctantly. 'There's a bit of a problem there.'

'Well, I can give you the money, no problem. I'm sure you're better with this stuff anyway – I never did get the hang of this new money.'

Billy had no idea what Grandpop was talking about. 'No, Grandpop, the thing is, you see – there's no way I'm allowed to buy tobacco. You have to prove you're over 16.'

'And if you say it's for your old Grandpop?'

'No way.'

'Preposterous! Oh well, vile as it may be, it looks like we'll both have to dive in and take the flak!'

At the entrance to Tesbury's hundreds of trolleys were lined up with a notice proclaiming: "We have twenty-three different types of trolley to make your shopping easier." There were trolleys for every different combination of babies and children imaginable, trolleys with special sections for baguettes and bottles of wine and probably trolleys with a built-in navigation system.

'Bit of a shame that there aren't any of those wire baskets but at least they've got one with a nifty canine jump-seat,' remarked Grandpop, pulling out a trolley with a blue plastic baby-seat and lifting Monty into it. 'Splendid view, eh, old boy?'

Billy didn't really want to say anything but his heart sank as a dishevelled-looking young mother with an exhausted expression on her face and a bouncy, newly-walking baby girl approached.

'Wow-wow!' exclaimed the little girl, excitedly pointing at Monty. 'Wow-wow! Loey wan'!'

The tired young mother seemed to be using the last of her energy to keep Chloe from climbing onto the trolley to claim Monty as the new addition to her cuddly toy collection and Billy noticed that they seemed to have picked exactly the one trolley from the twenty-three types that was right for Chloe.

'Um, Grandpop,' Billy muttered in Grandpop's ear. 'I think we'd better give up Monty's jump-seat to this little girl.'

'Oh, but of course! Bagging someone else's kite definitely not on! Here you are, young ladies, and do fly carefully!' Grandpop smiled and lifted Monty out. This was almost too much for Chloe, who clapped her hands excitedly. 'Wow-wow! Wow-wow! Loey wan'!' she shouted breathlessly.

It was almost too much for Monty, too, who joined in the fun by giving Chloe a playful lick across the face. As Billy and Grandpop found another trolley, the harassed young mother rustled worriedly around in a huge baby-changing rucksack, found a packet of wipes, and painstakingly wiped both Chloe's face and the trolley's child seat.

Ignoring the "No dogs" sign, Grandpop pushed Monty in the trolley, closely followed by Billy, into Tesbury's. Turning sharply past the greetings cards and the display of birthday cakes decorated with purple ponies, Grandpop arrived at the wrong end of the cash till. The lady on the till was holding a rather long and pointless conversation with her customer about the delightful canapés one could make with the bruised rocket that she'd just bought and had she tried the Blue Congo potatoes yet?

'Rockets? Congo? Sounds like a job for Johnny Walker,' Grandpop sniggered to Billy. 'Ah, good day to you, Madam. I would like four ounces of Wills' very best Virginia tobacco, if you please.'

'You'll find our selection of cigarettes, cigars, cigarillos and tobaccos over there,' the cashier indicated the counter with a beaming smile, and went back to chatting about wild raspberry balsamic vinegar.

At the cigarette and tobacco stand, a young man eventually found the tobacco and handed it over to Grandpop. 'Don't get much call for that brand these days mate,' said the young man, with a conspiratorial grin. 'And, by the way – just as a tip, dogs aren't really allowed, you know.'

'Good Heavens, my dear fellow!' exclaimed Grandpop. 'It's for me, not for old Monty here. Now, he might well want to retrieve my pipe if I hurled it somewhere but I very much doubt he'd want a puff himself! Now, there are a number of other items that maybe you'd be so good as to fetch for me. Corned beef, four tins. Fish paste, two jars. Salmon. Peek Freans…'

The young man chortled theatrically. 'That's a good one, mate! Bit of a joker, aren't you! But seriously, perhaps I can interest you in our Home Shopping service. Great for discerning time-poor customers like yourself, mate. Costs fifty a month and then 12 ½ % or thirty a month and 11 % if you've got one of our payback Ambrosia Supersaver cards or twenty a month and 10 ½ % if you've got your payback card *and* sign up now for our Friends & Family Broadband service. What d'you say?'

'I'd say that sounds somewhat surplus to requirements, thank you all the same. Good day to you.' Grandpop answered politely and steered the trolley away into the overloaded aisles in the great cavern that was Tesbury's.

Things actually improved as Billy, Grandpop and Monty hit the self-service section of Tesbury's. Billy managed to find most of the tins of that and jars of the other, Monty enjoyed the ride and Grandpop managed not to upset the Tesbury's system for at least five minutes. All they got were a few bemused looks.

But then Grandpop began insisting that they had to get a particular brand of biscuits in a tin that Billy had never heard of. They had to be those particular biscuits, because they were the tastiest thing in the world and Grandpop could not live without them (although Billy kept reminding him that he was meant to be dead). And they had to be in a tin because the tin was going to come in jolly useful wherever it was in the jungle they were off to.

'I don't think there are that many biscuits in tins, these days, Grandpop,' said Billy, secretly wishing that Grandpop would settle for some Tesbury's "Our Supreme Better than Best Selection" biscuits in a packet.

'Don't give up now, old chap! Can't have you losing your bottle when we're in the jungle. Let's ask this good fellow here!'

Grandpop approached a nervous-looking youth in a Tesbury's overall who was peering at a display of Cajun Spicy Rub with rightful confusion.

'Oh, hello there,' said the youth. 'My name's Cameron and I'm your Tesbury Find 'n' Help today. What can I find or how can I help?'

'Well, I'd be most grateful if you could point me in the right direction for the Peek Freans Family Assortment tins.'

'Tins? What are those exactly? Freak Beans or what you said? I'm really sorry, it's my first morning and...'

'Biscuits, Mr Cameron, biscuits. Where are they, please?'

'Oh, right, biscuits!' said Cameron brightly and led Grandpop, Billy and the trolley on what was to be something of a wild goose-chase around Tesbury's. 'Oh yes, biscuits. Did them on the last day of my training. They're just round here by the confectionary – oh, no, they done some re-merchandising since then. They should be by the breakfast cereals, if you'll just follow me – oh, no, they're renovating that aisle, we'll have to go round the other way – that's where they should be. Oh, I forgot, we've got the eleven-for-the-price-of-ten promotion there...'

As Billy and Grandpop tried to keep up with Cameron's twists and turns around the aisles and freezer cabinets of Tesbury's, Billy noticed that someone was following them with intent. It was the manic car washer, brandishing one of his sponges.

'...hold on a minute...please...on my lunch break just now,' spluttered the car washer. 'I just want to know – is that a 1959 or a 1960? Could I possibly...?'

And, if that wasn't bad enough, Billy suddenly noticed something flashing out of the corner of his other eye. Mrs Baby Pink Tracksuit had been joined by two friends in pastel. All three of them were holding up their mobile phones to take photos of Grandpop, in a confusion of false nails, jangly bracelets and sparkling wine-fuelled giggles.

'Ooh!' shrieked one of the women. 'He looks even better than he did in "Hello!" Real bit of trouser-totty, that is! Go on, Sharon, I dare you to get his autograph...'

They all converged upon Grandpop, Billy and Monty. And just as Cameron finally came to a stop in front of the dog biscuits section, Billy heard a piercing scream:

'Noooooooo! Wow-wow way! Loey wan'!'

The poor young mother approached at speed, pushing a trolley full of baby food, nappies, wipes, cuddly toys, pink T-shirts, organic apple juice, dummies, Baby Einstein DVDs, purple pony yoghurts and a distraught, red-faced Chloe, determined to get her hands on Monty.

Grandpop took one look at the procession in pursuit of his car, his dog, his trousers and goodness knows what else and calmly said to Billy:

'Sometimes a fellow's simply got to bail out. Kindly hand me the kaleidoscope, old chap!'

THE BROUHAHA AT BLUEY'S

By S. P. Moss

Everything began to spin around as Billy and Grandpop fell forward in time, whirling and drifting through seasons and decades, through wooden changing huts and old petrol stations and smiling tearooms. But slowly, the glimpses grew garish and unfriendly – neon coloured plastic and artificial hot-house plants. The smells that assailed Billy's nostrils were harsh and unpleasant – cheap perfume and aftershave, air freshener and nappies that needed changing.

As the spinning slowed and Billy came to his senses, he realised where he was, and it was somewhere he didn't particularly want to be – "Bluey's", a huge themed pool and water slide complex. He'd been there a couple of times and not particularly enjoyed it and as he came to a standstill, he remembered why.

"Bluey" was a cartoon dolphin with Hawaiian flowered-patterned skin, a surfboard, an Australian hat with corks hanging from in and a particularly dim grin. Bluey's pool and slide complex was under cover, which was ludicrous during the summer. The atmosphere was stifling and oppressive and not helped by the fact that the place was always crammed full of bodies. These bodies, men, women and children, were mostly unhealthy and pasty-looking. Many had piercings in strange places or spots (also in strange places.) Grown men in huge boxer trunks with overhanging bellies lumbered around, legs wide apart and feet splayed out. Blubbery women with bits wobbling all over the place were squeezed into tiny sequinned pink bikinis that looked as if they had been made for Barbie. Almost everyone in Bluey's looked and moved like an overgrown baby.

Billy glanced at his side to see Grandpop, also coming to his senses and eyeing Bluey's with distaste. The two of them were standing in between the baby pool, which was full of bright pink plastic Hawaiian flowers with faces on them and a children's "soft dry play area" which was called "Blue's Happy Crew Playpen". On the walls were posters in day-glo green and orange advertising "Bluey's Happy Crewsers" – some sort of swim nappies.

Grandpop marched briskly over towards the poster and stood, staring at all the neon and cartoon packets and advertising gibberish, his hands on his hips.

'What in Heaven's name is this place?' asked Grandpop, shaking his head. 'A swimming pool or a giant advertisement? I suppose, now that we're here, we should try to enjoy ourselves, eh, old chap? What else is there on offer for those out of nappies?'

On the way up towards some steps, from where one could get a bird's eye view of the entire complex, they passed various signs which all seemed to be telling people what they should try or definitely not even think about trying:

"Why not try a bite to eat at Bluey's Tucker Box? Your Healthy Options today are…"

"All children under 12 must be supervised *at all times.*"

"Danger! Any surface which is wet will be more slippery than any surface which is dry."

"This is the way to The Changing Village. Do not follow unless you intend to change." 'I assume they mean your ways,' Grandpop muttered.

"Thrills unlimited in Bluey's Wild Water Flumes. No diving or jumping."

The sight of numerous podgy vacant-expression people jammed into giant rubber rings bobbing around pointlessly did not really seem to live up to the description of "thrills" or "wild".

"You are advised to ride in such a position so you can see where you are going." 'Hmmm,' commented Grandpop. 'Helps sometimes with flying, too.'

'What shall we try, then, Grandpop?' asked Billy. He couldn't for the life of him imagine Grandpop crammed into a rubber ring or tucking into whatever Your Healthy Options were – it was unlikely that these would include Pink Gin.

'Well, it does occur to me that we've been grounded for rather a spell,' answered Grandpop 'perhaps one of those tower and slide jobbies might give us a little taste of being up there again – you know, flying?'

Grandpop and Billy headed off to climb the tower to "The Black Hole." This was reputedly the steepest of the slides on offer and the fact that the name had absolutely nothing to do with Bluey was reassuring. There were all sorts of signs and warnings on the way up including one that stated that the slide was "not to be used by pregnant women and people with back, neck and heart conditions."

'Does that include being deceased, so to say?' mused Grandpop.

Slightly more worrying for Billy were the continual reminders that "The Black Hole" slide was absolutely not to be used by anyone under thirteen. Grandpop seemed blithely unaware, as usual, but after the twentieth or so sign to this effect, Billy expressed his worry to Grandpop.

'You're not frightened, are you, old chap? I can't believe that for an instant – after braving time travel, a crocodile-infested lake, an Indian cobra and Oswald Featherstonehaugh, I would doubt that anything in this giant bath toy could frighten you!'

'It's not that…' whispered Billy as they neared the top of the steps. 'It's just that – I don't want to get into any trouble.'

'Oh, come on! What are they going to do, old chap? Ask you to produce your birth certificate on the spot? I'll deal with any problems, should they arise.'

Grandpop's way of dealing with problems in the 21st century was exactly what Billy was afraid of but he was really excited about the prospect of "The Black Hole". He'd desperately wanted a go last time he was here, having found the slide for 8+ rather tame.

"The Black Hole" was not bad at all, as far as water-slides go. First, you whizzed down a dark tunnel, disorientated by flashing lights and weird echoing sounds. Then you were flung around a sort of speedway-type track and finally deposited, in whatever position you ended up, in a large pool of water. It was all rather like being in a giant toilet. Luckily, this idea had not occurred to Bluey's, or else the ride would have been sponsored by some or other toilet paper brand.

Grandpop also seemed to enjoy the ride, despite himself. 'Jolly good fun, this giant khazi!' he shouted. 'Shall we have another go, for the road, as it were?'

Billy was keen to have another go but had been slightly alarmed by a frightening, thuggish-looking life guard who had eyed him suspiciously as he emerged from the giant toilet bowl. Billy hoped that the lifeguard would maybe go off and check that no-one was striding off to The Changing Village with absolutely no intention whatsoever of changing by the time they came down again. The two of them climbed to the top of the tower of stairs and positioned themselves at the top of "The Black Hole."

'Let's try it in tandem this time,' suggested Grandpop. 'Right! Chocks away!'

Billy knew that sliding in tandem was also something that one (or two) was strongly encouraged to not even think about trying. But he forgot his worries as the fun of the slide with its flashing lights took over.

But this time, as the two of them were spun into the landing pool, there was absolutely no doubt concerning the lifeguard's focus and intentions. He had called reinforcements and was now blowing furiously on his whistle, going red in the face. He gestured wildly to Billy and Grandpop to come to him and his colleagues. Wet, dripping and rather surprised, Grandpop and Billy made their way over to the group of lifeguards.

'Are you off your trolley, mate?' The big lifeguard shouted at Grandpop, veins rising on his temples, chest nearly bursting out of his Blue's Crew T-Shirt.

'Trolley,' muttered Grandpop aside to Billy. 'Wasn't that the problem at that frightful Tesbury's place?' He drew himself up smartly, swept the wet hair out of his eyes and stretched out his hand to the quivering lifeguard:

'Squadron Leader Walker. Good day. Now, what seems to be the problem?'

'The problem is, mate, that I seen you frew our

surveillance camera at the top of the Black Hole here with this kid – who I don't believe is thirteen, by the way – and you deliberately went down the ride together which is strickly prohibited. Strickly. How old are you?' He turned aggressively to Billy.

'Errm...you mean last birthday?' Billy didn't want to lie.

'Now look here, my good man. I can explain. You are quite right in thinking that Billy here is under thirteen. But I gave him my permission to ride on the slide here. As a responsible grown-up, I assessed the risks and made a judgement that the fun he'd have would far outweigh any highly unlikely downsides. I take full responsibility...'

'Yeah, but that's the whole point mate! You can't take responsibility. You can't go round making your own decisions on stuff here. What you just done is so bleedin' dangerous...'

'That is your opinion, my good man. I can assure you that your "Black Hole" here hardly rates high on the danger scale of what Billy has been up to recently, which has included piloting a Sunderland Flying Boat, paddling through a crocodile-infested lake...'

'You whaaat?' screeched the lifeguard.

'...and coming face to face with an Indian cobra...'

'Oh, come off it – I wasn't born yesterday!' The lifeguard obviously had a short attention span and was now bored with Grandpop's stories.

'...not to mention detonating a home-made bomb...'

'Get out! Get out and go! We've got you now on CCTV mate, and if you ever show your face here again…'

'That is highly unlikely. Good day to you. Come on Billy, let's get back to Monty and the car – and, by the way,' Grandpop looked at the exasperated lifeguard and winked conspiratorially 'I wasn't born yesterday, either. In fact, I was born in 1930!' And with that, Grandpop marched coolly and smartly off in the direction of The Changing Village, leaving the lifeguard aghast.

Just as Billy and Grandpop reached the door of The Changing Village, they were accosted again, this time by Bluey himself (or at least, some poor sweaty student squashed into a giant Bluey costume.)

'G'day and congratulations, cobbers. You are the 10,000th visitors to Bluey's. Step this way please to have your photo taken for the local paper. And your names are?' The creature spoke in a muffled and not very convincing Australian accent and attempted to put a stiff flipper over Billy's shoulder.

Grandpop closed his eyes and inhaled. He looked as if he was going to stretch out his arm to take one of the creature's flippers, but then thought better of it. 'Look here, dear chap,' he said, quietly but firmly 'much as it is a great honour, Billy and I are in a bit of a rush. I have to get back to base. Could you not perhaps do all the publicity with the 10,001st visitors just for once?'

'Oh, no, cobber!' the dolphin exclaimed. 'At Bluey's Rules is Rules! Come this way, sir!'

'Oh, good grief!' Grandpop grabbed Billy and dragged him through the door of The Changing Village. Bluey tried to follow, but this was simply not possible in a seven foot high dolphin costume.

Outside, away from the sweaty bodies and oppressive

heat, rules and regulations of Bluey's, it was pleasantly warm in the fresh air, with a little breeze. Billy and Grandpop found the Austin Healey parked in a vaguely familiar spot in the car park. Monty had been waiting patiently but started yapping happily when he saw Grandpop and Billy returning. He jumped out of the car, almost turning a somersault in his excitement.

'I think our best plan is to drop you back where I picked you up. At the bend in the road, by Gran. Then I can make my exit unobtrusively. With the minimum of fuss and bother,' said Grandpop.

It sounded a good plan but like most of Grandpop's plans in the 21st century, it was not to be. Just as Billy was about to get into the car, the overgrown schoolboy car washer from Tesbury's popped up, sponge and bucket at the ready, his over keen face beaming:

'Oh, please can I wash your car, sir? It would be a pleasure, a real pleasure. I haven't seen one of these for twenty years and it always was my dream. I collect Dinky Toy boxes and I have one, an original from 1959, in A-1 condition – a box that is – only the model featured is red and not the British Racing Green – I'd do it for free, you know, I've followed you all the way here from Tesbury's!' The man started to brandish his sponge on the paintwork.

'Now, that's terribly kind of you my man, but it won't be necessary. I really do have to leave…' Grandpop climbed into the car. Billy's way was blocked by the eager car washer and his bucket.

'Excuse me, please…' Billy mumbled weakly, trying to get into the car.

'Oh, good God!' Grandpop exclaimed. Billy looked up

towards Bluey's. Emerging from Bluey's was Bluey himself, accompanied by huge numbers of balloons with 10,000 on them, a woman with a microphone and a man with an alarmingly large camera.

'Hold it just there, cobbers!' All seven foot of Bluey plus balloons stomped down toward the little car.

Suddenly Billy heard a screech of brakes behind them. He turned to see a huge tank of a 4x4 park and spew out its contents of a gaggle of silly giggling women who were old enough to know better. They tottered out with much fluffing up of hair, jangling of bracelets and tapping of false nails on mobile phones.

Billy groaned. It really was embarrassing – they were all old enough to be his mother. 'I think it's your fan club, Grandpop,' he muttered. They could now hear snatches of the conversation:

'Oooh, there he is! Drop dead gorgeous or what!'

'Has he got Sierra with him?'

'Oh, he's not going out with *her* any more. She's history…now, Carrie, darling, wouldn't you say this is the biggest scoop you've ever had?'

Alarmed, Billy now recognised one of the women as Carrie de Winter, the famous newsreader and Josh's mother. As the women giggled their way nearer, Billy was also aware of the car washer with his sponge still at the ready, to his right. And to his left, Bluey the giant dolphin plus entourage was beating an unstoppable path to Billy, Grandpop, Monty and the Austin Healey Sprite.

'Oh, good Heavens above! Why does there always have to be such a song and dance any time we try to drive anywhere here?' Grandpop leaned over to Billy, who'd meanwhile slipped into the car. He laid his hand over Billy's and drummed his fingers a little, then clasped Billy's hand in his. 'Sorry old chap, but you're going to have to give me the kaleidoscope. A man's gotta do and all that. And you run. Just run. There will be enough fireworks going on here that they won't notice you.'

As he fumbled in his rucksack, Billy could hear a muddle of voices increasing in volume – an over-enthusiastic voice, a fake jokey Australian voice and a muddle of giggling shrieking mutton dressed as lamb voices. A last lick from Monty and Billy passed Grandpop the kaleidoscope, like a relay baton. He looked into Grandpop's brave and cheery blue eyes for the last time.

'Grandpop, that was all – wizard!'

CONNECT ONLINE

If you enjoyed **GURNARDS'S BOOK OF DELIGHTS**, please write a review or connect online. Thank you.

STORIES FOR CHILDREN

www.kids4books.blogspot.co.uk/

VANESSA WESTER:

Main Blog

www.vanessawesterwriter.blogspot.co.uk/

Twitter

www.twitter.com/vanessa_wester/

S.P. MOSS:

Website

www.burmeon.com

Made in the USA
Charleston, SC
05 July 2013